To Paul Bernius
daughter:
    Sister Maureen
Bernius — S.C.
with affectionate Regard

Jeanne Toomey

ASSIGNMENT HOMICIDE
Behind the Headlines

JEANNE TOOMEY

Jeanne Toomey

Sunstone books may be purchased for educational, business, or sales promotional use.
For information please write: Special Markets Department,
Sunstone Press, P.O. Box 2321, Santa Fe, New Mexico 87504-2321.

FIRST EDITION

10 9 8 7 6 5 4 3 2 1

Library of Congress Cataloging in Publication Data:
Toomey, Jeanne, 1921–
    Assignment homicide: a newspaper sage / by Jeanne Toomey.—1st ed.
    p. cm.
    ISBN: 0-86534-271-7
    1. Toomey, Jeanne, 1921– . 2. Women journlists—New York (State)—New York—
Biography. I. Title.
PN4874. T624A94   1998
070' .92—dc21
[B]   98-35870
                                                                CIP

Published by SUNSTONE PRESS
            Post Office Box 2321
            Santa Fe, NM 87504-2321 / USA
            (505) 988-4418 / *orders only* (800) 243-5644
            FAX (505) 988-1025

Dedicated in gratitude to Sam Rubenstein.
He was always like a father to me.

FOREWORD

TO THE EXTENT THAT ONE JOURNALIST'S experience is much like another's, this memoir in many ways duplicates the lives of thousands of others who I hope will see something of themselves in its pages, and smile.

Many of my friends and mentors died without telling their stories. This book in a modest way intends to remember some of the greatest journalists who ever lived during an era when newspapers flourished in the greatest city of the world, New York (including its biggest borough, Brooklyn). As possibly the only, or else one of the very few surviving founders of the New York Press Club (and the only woman founder), I'd like to tell a few of their stories, mindful of Ben Hecht's comment, "We write each other's obits and they're gawdamighty brief."

Freddy Anderson, baldheaded court reporter for the *Brooklyn Daily Eagle*, often told of being taken to the ball game by his father in Williamsburg.

"Daddy, what do these men do for a living?" he asked.

"Why, Son, they're professionals."

"You mean, they get paid for playing ball!"

And that's what newspapering has been for many of us, being paid for "playing ball."

One of the best aspects of reporting is simply being outdoors. Before being hired by my first of scores of newspapers, I had had my share of dull office jobs. At twenty-one, to be cooped up all day in a hot, stuffy office was a grind.

The last such post I was to have, squeezed in briefly between Cardozo and Nathan and the *Brooklyn Daily Eagle*, was for a dignified biographical encyclopedia, J. T. White and Company, then located at the Educational Building, Twelfth Street and Fifth Avenue, New York.

Men who could sell, but not write, went around the country interviewing recent widows. For a thousand dollars, which included an etching of the deceased spouse, they could have a biography of their late husband included, no matter what his accomplishments (or lack of them).

One day fine snow was turning the city into a mirage of lighted towers, softening the outlines, turning the bare trees into white ghosts, and I was in the office of J. T. White and Company, looking out the window. Fire bells were ringing and the great red engines passed under the window.

That did it, and I quit. I felt almost physically that everyone out there was alive, pulsating, on the way to exciting adventures, and I was cooped indoors with a library full of books about people no one else had ever heard of.

"But you have security here," said the kindly J. T. White descendant, still running the publishing house established by a shrewd ancestor wise to the ways of human vanity.

"I don't want security. I want a newspaper job," was my reply. Now, more than half a century later, I still think that was a good answer, one maybe more young people should make, if not for a newspaper job, at least for a career they will actually enjoy if they don't want to end up in some dreary, dead-end slave ship, mummified with boredom.

CODE OF SILENCE

"Rosa, don't talk!"

"Tony, don't talk!"

Mothers were calling down to their children on the street as the bloody body of Anthony Imperiale lay in the courtyard of a tenement on Madison Street on New York's Lower East Side.

An orange harvest moon lit up the dark street. It was Halloween, 1943. Youngsters dressed as skeletons, pirates and ghosts ran into the entrance without stopping. This was one of my first New York murder scenes and also my introduction to *omerta*. I was to encounter it often again in decades of seeing murder up front.

A similar incident was immortalized in a photograph taken from a tenement roof by the celebrated Weegee. Heads hung out from every window. Residents would not speak to the police, but they were all looking down at the corpse of a former resident sprawled on the ground. Weegee called it "Front Row at a Murder." The photograph hung on a wall in the reporters' shack in back of Manhattan headquarters. The number four—Four Centre Market Place—seemed apt for its occupants, all members of the Fourth Estate.

Weegee slept in a rusted car outside of the press shack with the police radio on day and night. Though dirty, unshaved and eccentric, the man was an undoubted genius. Books and movies have immortalized him and his work. His documentary on the San Gennaro Festival on Mulberry Street became a classic.

THE BLOODY DEUCES

Mulberry Street, which runs parallel to and in back of or east of Centre Market Place where the Manhattan reporters' shack used to be, was and still is the address of many great Italian restaurants like Angelo's as well as wonderful bakeries and stores selling religious articles. A tenement at 222 Mulberry Street known as "The Bloody Deuces" was said to have been the location of more murders than any other building in New York. The murders dated back to the nineteenth century when the Black Hand, or Unione Siciliane, ruled Mulberry Street as its descendant, the Mafia, was to do in my time.

When I took the IRT to Brooklyn that spring day more than half a century ago, I had no way of knowing that my real professional life was about to begin. I didn't have a bat and gloves but I carried a notebook and pen—the only tools I would need for many years.

My arrival in Brooklyn began in a mixup which seemed a prophetic starting point to my near decade on the only major daily being published in the Borough of Churches.

Though I asked directions, I found myself on Johnson Avenue, not Johnson Street, in a grey industrial region with no roaring presses.

But an electric sign gave the welcome information: BAR—The Ear Muff Cafe. I headed there.

When a customer started into his family problems or financial troubles and the bartender had had enough, he'd just cut short the sad tale of domestic infelicity or economic woe by ringing up No Sale and donning a pair of earmuffs.

"Where's Johnson Street, Sir?" I screamed over the earmuffs so he could hear me.

He patiently doffed his plaid earmuffs to give me correct directions. "Downtown Brooklyn," he told me, gesticulating in a vaguely southern direction. "Take the IRT, not the Independent Subway. You're on the outskirts of Queens!"

I headed off on yet another subway to 24 Johnson Street near Brooklyn Borough Hall and my first newspaper job.

BROOKLYN SHACK

World War II was raging in various theatres in Europe, Asia and North Africa. In the year or two following Pearl Harbor, ten million young men had donned uniforms and newspapers were crying for help. The only pool of prospective employees left was women, which is why I and a group of other young women were hired. Active young male reporters and copyreaders were at war.

The date was April 17, 1943 when I started work in the big fourth floor City Room, typing up reams of a wartime feature called "With Our Servicemen." My next assignment came in July, three months later, and took me out of the *Eagle* City Room.

"Take the IRT to Bergen Street," City Editor Ed Wilkinson ordered. "You'll see a big grey stone building, Brooklyn Police Headquarters. Our office is just across the street. Go in and introduce yourself. The guys will show you the ropes. You'll be the only girl."

It was a golden day of full summer. Children were running in the streets, police cars were parked in parallel rows in front of the massive grey stone building which had two green lights in front of it.

Bergen Street was sleeping in the strong July sun when I arrived, but underneath the surface was a humming sense of expectancy, of manuscripts of death, despair and high hilarity.

Across from the grim-looking rock fortress were two nondescript store fronts topped by a decaying apartment house. The overall color of the buildings was a blotchy yellow. Here the police reporters occupied a kind of field camp operated by the major new York dailies and the *Brooklyn Daily Eagle*. It was called the "Brooklyn Shack."

On Sixth Avenue in the heart of Park Slope, the Shack was at the apex of a triangle formed by Sixth Avenue, Flatbush Avenue and Bergen Street. Though a prosaic blue-collar area, it all looked dazzling, mysterious, exciting, full of promise to me. And so it proved to be. No more dull offices, columns of figures, clipping the *Law Journal*. I had arrived at my true home. And best of all, I had realized my dream of covering crime rather than tea parties, often the fate of female reporters.

There were a few company names on the store window of the humble cubicle where I was to work for several years. The gold-lettered signs read: *The New York Times, New York Herald-Tribune*, Standard News Association and *Brooklyn Daily Eagle*. Only the *Times* is still in business.

OFFICE MATES

"I'm Sam Rubenstein," a middle-aged, stocky black-haired man, conservatively dressed for the area in a neat reddish-brown and cream checked cotton jacket, white shirt, yellow silk tie and dark brown trousers, announced with a big smile.

"And this is the *New York Times* man, Manny Perlmutter," he went on. "Your desk is right in the middle, facing the door. I sit opposite Manny so I can keep an eye on him," he said with a chuckle.

I liked him right away. He had a thoroughly professional yet kindly paternal attitude to me throughout my years at Bergen Street.

Sam, who was also called Ruby by many of his colleagues, worked for Standard News Association and the *New York Herald-Tribune*. Sam's son, Howard Rubenstein, was to become the most famous and successful press agent and lobbyist in America with McDonald's just one of his accounts, as well as the Uniformed Firefighters and other municipal unions, the governor, the Empire State Building, Donald Trump, Duchess of York Sarah Ferguson, the hit plays, and a vast number of top hotels, restaurants and other real estate and political accounts.

A good-looking blue-eyed slightly younger man, Manny was a sporty dresser, given to sharp checks and bow ties, who looked like and turned out to be a horse player.

Manny was a graduate of New York University who had beaten the odds of a youth spent in Brownsville where his family ran a small shop on Sheffield Avenue selling newspapers, candy and cigarettes. Many of his childhood friends ended in the electric chair.

Though educated and well mannered, Manny sometimes reverted to the speech and gags of his origin.

Extra assignments caused him to mutter, "I'm going to leave my fly open. If they're going to work me like a horse, I might just as well look like one." The thought of the *New York Times* Brooklyn Shack reporter appearing at 229 West Forty-Third Street thus exposed made me giggle. Of course, he never did.

For many years we three were to share a tiny office, not much bigger than a hall bedroom or shed. There were three scarred desks, three worn chairs and one leather lounge chair with a broken arm which served as a cot for some of our more disreputable colleagues on the night side.

Though there was a telephone booth-sized privy in a corner, I never entered it, going across the street to the policewomen's lavatory or a local bar instead.

After a brief chat with Manny Perlmutter, Sam told me he would introduce me to the other reporters assigned to the Shack. The names, including Sam Rubenstein, Emanuel Perlmutter, Harry T., Charles and John Feeney, Irving Lieberman, Joseph Kahn, Travis Fulton, Michael O'Brien and Joseph Kiernan were familiar to me because I saw their bylines almost daily in the great dailies which in the forties served New Yrok.

Sam led me next door to the other ground floor office, that of the *New York Post*.

"This is Jeanne Toomey, the new *Brooklyn Eagle* reporter," Sam told the occupant. "And this is the man with the best files on Brooklyn murders in the world, Irving Lieberman."

"Nice to meet you. Good luck here," said the *Post* man with a pleasant smile and wave. He was barricaded before a huge, old-style rolltop desk.

"The *Post* sent him that desk, a personal gift from Dorothy Schiff," Sam said as he led me to a stairway. "Mrs. Schiff is the publisher. Irving is very well thought of."

As he spoke, he opened a door revealing a battered-looking flight of stairs. "The *Daily News* office is up a few steps, on the right, and the *World-Telegram*, *Sun* and *Mirror* are up a flight, too, but on your left," he went on.

He reached a landing, turned left, and led me into a large sunny office overlooking Brooklyn Headquarters, which also contained the 78th Precinct. There was a cot inside the door against the wall, partly shielded by long red velvet portieres. A large grey and white cat could be glimpsed asleep on the cot. Further down the long room were several desks. There was a royal flush framed on the wall with a notation giving the date when Harry Feeney had won it.

"Jeanne, I want you to meet the three Feeneys, Harry, John and Charley," said Sam. "And this gentleman is Jesse Strait. He's a great photographer with the *Mirror*." Strait, who was rather formally dressed in a dark suit, a grey fedora and a black coat, stood up and shook hands.

The brothers turned around, looked me over and nodded pleasantly.

Charley, who I learned later was the Bergen Street "pipe artist," gave me a warm grin and said, "They sent Dorothy Kilgallen down here to break in and when she got to be famous, she forgot all about us. Are you going to be like that?"

"No, and if I ever get back to law school and become a lawyer, I'll represent you for nothing," I told him. (Lack of tuition had forced me to drop out of Fordham Law School. There was no federal student loan program in the forties.)

I found out later that no reporter would need my anticipated services since the local lawyers loved to represent them for free publicity, usually arranged by Sam Rubenstein, who numbered among his clients a future Surrogate, District Attorney and many judges.

Sam smiled and led me out into the hall and then up a few stairs to another office where I met Mike O'Brien and Joe Kiernan of the *New York Daily News*. There were brief greetings and we returned downstairs to our office, as I now thought of 66 Sixth Avenue.

A ONE-MAN BUREAU

Sam was an astonishing man. He somehow managed to carry on a busy public relations business while continuing to be a top reporter. And he had two reporting jobs, working for the *Herald-Tribune* as his main affiliation and also Standard News Association, a kind of local version of the Associated Press or City News.

A down-to-earth strategist, Sam always said, "Make friends!" He sure made a friend of me.

One day he came over and said, "Jeanne, I want you to come with me to the Girls Club of Brooklyn tonight and write a story about it for the *Eagle*."

"Oh, I couldn't do that, Mr. Rubenstein," I told him. "I don't think Mr. Schroth [the publisher] would like that."

Sam looked at me, probably praying for patience. "How much do you make a week?" he asked me.

"Twenty-seven fifty a week," I told him.

Sam handed me fifty dollars and repeated, "I want you to come with me to the Girls Club of Brooklyn tonight and write a story about it for the *Eagle*!"

I did it. Soon Sam began to turn over Catholic accounts like Saint Joseph College for Women and the Knights of Columbus Carnival to me.

He also handed me big steaks from his Fort Greene Meat Market account.

I brought them back to my surrogate family, the Henschels. I lived with them at 134 Lafayette Avenue in Brooklyn's Hill section after a former Greenwich Village roommate, Shirley Krasnoff, left virtuoso musician Blanche Krell and me to pursue a master's degree in sociology at Ohio State.

Molly Henschel refused to let me pay for my board and room and I tried to make up for this by turning my ration books over to her, plus Sam's steaks. The daughter of the family, Virginia Henschel, was and still is my closest friend.

Sam Rubenstein occasionally encountered jealousy from reporters who resented his common sense, most of all that he was making money as a press agent while doing a more than conscientious job as a reporter. A diplomat, he managed to juggle both occupations, succeeding brilliantly in each.

Even those who initially disliked him were almost always soon won over. Adelphi Hospital was one of his accounts. He arranged for babies to be born there *pro bono* and for some reporters' hapless relatives to get critical operations there, also totally or partially on the cuff.

One morning when I came in, Sam shook a finger at me. "I'm disappointed in you, Jeanne," he said. "You got drunk yesterday. You'll ruin your future. Don't do it again!"

"Thanks, Sam. I'll watch it," I said.

Though I felt hurt, I knew he was right. I cut down my intake—at least at Bergen Street. At twenty-one I was still growing up. Feelings of self-importance at working with all these men sometimes were mingled with fear of failure. Sam was kindly, reassuring and blessedly impersonal.

By returning good for evil, including brushing off anti-Semitic remarks, Sam Rubenstein built a legacy of good will, as well as exceptional skills, which his son carried on as—without doubt—the top press agent on the east coast, perhaps in the nation.

His kindness to a poor Irish kid made me Sam's grateful and respectful friend.

He had a kind of moral strength and wisdom which helped me, as well as everyone he interacted with on the police beat. I can still hear him saying, "I think I can develop this into a good story for the *Herald-Tribune*!" And he did just that—adding the flashes of color, the telling details, which transformed a routine police story into a form of art. His friendly yet sober and dignified ways caused people to open up to him, revealing the hidden motives and feelings which made a routine tale stirring.

"What's wrong with it?" Harry would snap on hearing Sam's plan to make it into a "good *Herald-Tribune* story."

A master diplomat, Sam would turn away wrath with a soothing compliment. "It's a fine story, Harry! Only you could have gotten that information from the cops," he would say. "I think it's great. I owe you one."

But once alone in our shabby home away from home, Sam would discreetly add the little touches and quotes that made his coverage of many a sordid tale into a true *Herald-Tribune* story, an "in-depth" feature, a work of art.

Joe Levy, who covered Cairo for the *Times* for twenty years, once summed up the *Tribune*'s special quality at a Newswomen's Ball: "To read the *Times* is a must. To read the *Tribune* is a pleasure."

Sam would also make things square with Harry Feeney by offering him a special news story he would manage to get from one of his contacts, something he knew would be of special interest to Harry's paper, the *New York World-Telegram*. One editor there was obsessed with traffic, including highways, routes and traffic lights and though Harry might groan, he knew that he would get high marks by offering this editor new developments in his area of special interest.

HARRY'S QUICK TEMPER

Harry Feeney was unequalled in his own way. He almost was a cop—could quote them exactly, thought like them and had many special "ins" or pull with the police. But he also had a short fuse. We were working hard on a major crime story one day when the late William T. Whalen, Chief of Detectives, a sociable police official who delighted in playing the piano at press parties, dropped by Harry's upstairs office on a friendly visit. Though Harry showed impatience, Whalen hung around too long.

"Get out of here or I'll print that your personal take is forty thousand a month," warned Harry. Whalen made a fast exit. We all knew that many of the police brass were venal, owning apartment houses in Miami and elsewhere. That administration was reputed to be notoriously corrupt, paving the way for the later Harry Gross investigation in Brooklyn which had cops diving out windows and going to jail. Gross was a bookie who paid cops off in the Dugout Bar near Ebbets Field where the Brooklyn Dodgers played ball.

Since the *Post* office, under the supervision of Irving Lieberman (better known as "The Mouse"), was next door to ours, Sam, Manny and I saw a lot of Irving.

He had a long nose and tiny bright eyes which may have won him his nickname. As Sam had pointed out while showing me around, Irving's file of known criminals and famous Brooklyn cases was a treasury which I hope has been saved. He was a thorough, careful newsman and later we saw Paris together with his nephew, Marvin, since we both got the dream assignment of covering the maiden voyage of the superliner S.S. *United States* in July 1952.

His cub, and my counterpart as a beginner, was Joe Kahn who, alas, died December 1st, 1997. We both started at Brooklyn Police Headquarters the same day. The police had a welcoming gambit for new police reporters. It was a large scrapbook showing horrible unretouched pictures of murder victims. We dutifully looked this over. Joe turned green and I helped him down the front steps. Despite this awkward start, we became fast friends.

The *Daily News* office, headed by Mike O'Brien, had few visitors. O'Brien was anti-Semitic, anti-black and anti- almost anything progressive. He had a Steeplechase ad grin, a shock of stiff white hair and was right out of *All in the Family*. The Feeneys took pleasure in constantly whacking him with exclusives. He sometimes got back at them. But since there were three of them and only one O'Brien, the score was generally on their side.

One exasperating *Journal-American* reporter, Emil Steinhauser, had been Brisbane's secretary and was farmed out at Bergen Street by the Hearst organization, much as another "Hearstling," Travis Fulton, was, to keep him on a payroll. He was apt to sabotage an interview by demanding an answer to some tactless question, resulting in all of us being shown the door.

"Are you now or have you ever been a Communist?" he demanded of a Board of Education official during the witch hunt days of Senator Joe McCarthy, promptly closing off any further communication.

When I berated him, he replied, "My office told me to ask that!"

"Yeah, but *later*, Emil, not at the start of the interview."

A TENEMENT FIRE

Initially I covered Brooklyn days and Manhattan Saturday nights. Later I was switched back and forth. On a Saturday night soon after my arrival at 4 Centre Market Place, the Manhattan Shack, a signal came over in Manhattan for a five-alarm fire. Running after the male reporters, I climbed over endless snake-like piles of hose on Mulberry Street. In the distance were the highest ladders the Fire Department possessed, propped against the walls of an old law tenement where stairs were still the only means of ascent. Flames were licking the black sky. It was around midnight. Firemen were carrying down children, aiding men and women in bedclothes, even carrying out dogs and cats. One uniformed man was carrying a bird cage.

I learned then why all the world loves a fireman. Duane Street firemen later gave me a big silver badge reading "Buff". Since I didn't wear a fedora like my male colleagues, I couldn't place a press card visibly in the band. This shiny silver badge, pinned to a dress or suit coat, got me through the lines.

DREAM ASSIGNMENT

Covering Manhattan Police Headquarters was exciting and demanding with murders, fires, bank holdups, traffic accidents and every kind of mayhem imaginable our daily fare. We listened to the police radio with its signals: 30 for a crime of violence, 32 for lesser crimes, 33 for endless car thefts. Bells rang constantly, giving the location of fires, and general commotion was the norm.

As a cub, I was expected to check everything and I busily did while some of my male peers got drunk at Headquarters Tavern down the street or cooked, if that was their specialty. John Rogan of the *Daily Mirror*, who came from Sheepshead Bay, often had fish cooking in his office. Sometimes, to my horror, in his *pot-au-feu* was a revolting sheep's head, complete with eyes.

I was convinced my male colleagues would eat anything if it were free, but I made no comment and tried to remain respectfully silent about my opinions for, make no mistake, these guys were superb reporters, masters of the craft, and they were generously teaching me their professional secrets.

The deliciously sultry Anne Viviani, good looking, elegant Maggie Bartel, and the sensitive and beautiful Edie Jackson (later Mrs. Jim Cahill, who invariably beat all the guys at Poker) were a few of the New York women reporters who occasionally covered Manhattan Headquarters. But I was the only female in the forties on regular day-to-day assignment there.

Edie Cahill later became an NBC television assignment editor for News Center Four, a true friend to her comrades-turned-press agents. Maggie Bartel, reportedly the first woman on the *New York Daily News* to cover hard news, was later anchorwoman for Congress Answers on WATV, Channel 13. She married Maurice "Moe" Kivel, a *New York Daily News* editor, and moved to Key West. Anne Viviani also married and I lost touch with her. These capable and talented women usually appeared when big stories were breaking.

The ever-present radio alarms and fire bells tipped us off that a crime or fire was underway.

One winter night an alarm reported a burglary in progress at a Grand Street down-at-the-heels bar and grill we sometimes frequented.

Ever the eager beaver, I led the pack into this gin mill just as two armed men were coming out, guns still visible in their hands. Diving under a table that had a red and white checked tablecloth on it, I stayed put until a cop looked underneath, reporting with a big grin, "They're gone. Come on out."

Feeling pretty silly, I reappeared. "Guess I jumped the gun," I mumbled.

Though the details have faded, I can still see that red and white tablecloth. Nothing was turned in on this, since we were totally out of order. Also, we had no desire to make our allies, the police, look foolish. In some ways police reporters became the partners of the police, almost cops with a notebook, since we were there all the time. Desk men or those on different beats were assigned investigations and "hatchet jobs" on New York's Finest.

In the Manhattan Shack the reporters were located just opposite the rear of New York's Police Headquarters at 240 Center Street. I shared a ground floor office with Artie Rosenfeld, a hardworking, sober reporter with the *New York Post*.

The police vans brought prisoners into our one-block street, Centre Market Place, and loaded them there to take them to court, down a few blocks at 100 Center Street.

THE ADONIS MURDER

"Who's that?" I asked a uniformed officer one morning as he shepherded a strikingly handsome blond man into a waiting van.

"Walter Dahl!"

I knew of this prisoner from the headlines.

Dahl was charged with the Adonis Torso murder. He and Solon Burt

Hargar, a ballroom dancer at the Plaza Hotel, were homosexual lovers. When Hargar, who was bisexual, announced plans to marry his gorgeous female dancing partner, police charged that Dahl killed him, sliced up the body in the kitchen of their apartment and dropped the parts off a Staten Island ferry boat.

After examining a part of the body that washed up on a Rockaway beach, destroying some bathers' summer, the medical examiner pronounced the remains to be those of a magnificently developed male athlete.

The newspapers took care of the rest, labeling the investigation "The Adonis Torso Case." A YMCA towel, used to wrap up body parts, led to the arrest of Dahl.

Another cutting and slicing case led merely to a petty Health Department complaint.

When a much-arrested criminal found his lover dead in their shabby DeKalb Avenue flat, he proceeded to cut her into parts. He stowed the gory remains in a locker at the Atlantic Avenue railroad station, causing grievous olfactory offense to the Salvation Army musicians who kept their trumpets in the next locker. They complained to the station authorities who, after a whiff or two, called the police.

Detectives carried the parts up to the street in suitcases. I went along, eyeing the cases and hoping I was imagining the more-than-musty odor. The light was out in the freight elevator and the rain beat down.

"The policeman's lot is not a happy one," I murmured.

As they stowed their find in a police van, I looked around. Atlantic Avenue, a dismal and dreary thoroughfare at best, was truly populated by lost souls that morning. A drunk in a torn yellow slicker weaved out of the Depot Bar. A stout lady in a many-colored mumu trotted alongside, holding a newspaper over her head, her dyed-blond hair writhing in curlers.

Curls of fog streamed in, blurring the street and traffic lights, leaving pools of rainbows on the drab streets.

But somehow, despite economic and social misery, there were fewer homeless on the streets then. All of the sad and hopeless yet seemed to have some burrow they called home.

I went back to Bergen Street and awaited the report from the morgue at Kings County Hospital.

Shortly after the discovery of the body parts, the medical examiner's office revealed that the woman had died of a heart attack. I pondered a real mystery. Why would some nitwit cut up someone who died of a heart attack?

Her imbecilic boyfriend was discovered washing dishes in a diner in Albany, and brought back to Brooklyn.

"Why did you cut your girlfriend up?" I asked, having obtained permission to interview him in the prisoner's cell in Brooklyn Felony Court.

"I got a long yellow sheet," (record of previous arrests), was his explanation.

"But didn't you know that on autopsy it would show that she died of natural causes?"

"So I didn't go to college! I figured the cops would blame me and arrest me for killing her."

Shaking my head, I reassured one of the world's consistent losers, a skinny rat-faced individual, that he only faced a very minor charge, a Sanitary Code violation for failing to dispose lawfully of a dead body.

QUEEN OF THE BOWERY

Joseph Mitchell, star of Scripps-Howard feature writers, included the story of Mazie, Queen of the Bowery in one of his marvelous collections of short stories about New York personalities and places.

I got a tip from Monroe Ehrman, the Voice of Coney Island, an old-style hardworking press agent, that Mazie had relocated and now reigned at the Speedway Scooter, 809 Surf Avenue in the heart of Coney Island. I sought her out.

"The Bowery's not the same anymore," she rasped. "They're tearing down everything, and the hobos have no place to go now. They're not bums, just forgotten men. A woman can always find some place to go, but a man—once he's down, he's down."

The blond lady who was cashier of the old Venice Theatre on the Bowery for thirty-five years was accepting the customers' cash at the scooter ride. She wore her trademark green plush top hat decorated with enough vegetables to make up a salad, a bright yellow coat and an old rose scarf embellished with sequins. Her shoes, of ersatz lizard, were high-heeled with ankle straps, decorated with flowers.

Mazie shrugged at her proximity to the Atlantic Ocean, outside her cashier's cage, dismissing the health benefits of fresh sea air and sunshine.

"I don't like Coney Island," she muttered resentfully. "I liked the Bowery.

Over there I helped them better. I'd find these men sleeping in a cellar, so dirty, and could take them out for coffee and a plate of soup." Though Mazie did not mention her many other acts of kindness to the derelicts she encountered, it was well known that she often gave them money for a "flop" and paid their court fines, too.

"In my time," she had told Mitchell when she was still impresario of the Venice Theatre at 209 Park Row, Manhattan, "I been as free with my dimes as old John D. himself."

In Coney Island, she had to content herself with handing out lollipops to the children who came for the scooter ride, and giving money to the occasional unfortunate who showed up at her window.

A few blocks from Mazie's new job location, a Coney Island blaze nearly cost me my *Brooklyn Eagle* job. I was in the City Room of the *Brooklyn Daily Eagle*, typing a story about a boy who killed his brother. The boy's last name was Good and he lived in Bushwick.

While I was writing the story, a Bergen Street friend called to tell me that Luna Park, a Coney Island amusement park, was on fire and the boys were "rolling" on it, meaning they were about to go.

I was appalled. Sam was off. He, of course, had gotten me my weekend job with the *Trib*, and unfortunately the *Eagle* had just changed my days off, having me work in the office part of the time before leaving for the Manhattan Shack. I was still listed as the *Trib*'s "Brooklyn man" Saturdays.

Earlier that summer I had even gone into the *Tribune* City Room, wearing a new suit and a big navy straw hat, to ask for a full-time job there. I carried my scrapbook with my best stories pasted in it. But once there, I was too nervous to walk up to the City Desk and apply. I didn't even look around to see if anyone I knew was there to introduce me.

I hoped to get my courage up and try again. So I hadn't yet notified them of my Saturday change of assignment, working in the *Eagle* office instead of at Bergen Street.

Under the desk, I called Pennsylvania 6-4000. When I told the *Trib* about the fire, the desk man said, "Of course, you're rolling on it!"

"Of course," I replied. When I hung up, I rushed into the office of the *Eagle*'s managing editor, Robert M. Grannis (later to join the *Pittsburgh Post-Gazette*), and breathlessly told him about the fire.

"I'd better go," I said.

But Grannis answered, "No. Finish the homicide, and I'll send Jaffe."

My ambition was to get a full-time job on the *Herald-Tribune*, for which I had a slavish admiration and respect. In fact, I loved the *Herald-Tribune* passionately, and later fell madly in love with Robert S. Bird, a *Tribune* star, maybe partly because he was a major writer for the *Herald-Tribune*. I once did a story about my desperate love affair with Bird called "A City Room Romance" and ran it in the "New York Column" when I was editor of that weekly.

But all that came later.

Reviewing my chances of landing a job on the *Tribune*, I reacted at the visceral level and just left. I sneaked through the morgue, around a long back corridor going by Publisher Frank D. Schroth's office and Executive Editor Edwin B. Wilson's office, both located, like the newsroom, on the fourth floor.

Taking the stairs, I landed in Flood Alley where the trucks parked, ran down the street and hailed a cab.

Speeding seventy miles an hour down the Belt Parkway towards Coney Island, I was wildly excited. As we neared Coney Island, I could see billowing smoke. A scenic railway twisted and turned in the blaze like a great *papier maché* snake.

"That's where we're going. I'm a reporter," I bragged to the cabbie.

He shook his head. "I ain't going too close," he said. "This crate of shit will blow up!"

He dumped me off two blocks away and I ran the rest of the way. It was a superb fire. No one got killed or even hurt. Mayor Fiorello La Guardia, Fire Commissioner Patrick Walsh and other regulars at big fires were all there. I interviewed everybody, helped out a new *Herald-Tribune* man, Lawrence Thompson (later to join the *Miami Herald*) and finally, covered with smoke, my stockings in ladder, with smudges on my face and neck, I returned to the *Eagle* by subway since I didn't have enough cash for a cab back.

(Thompson was destined to join the *Miami Herald* after a *Herald-Tribune* operator snitched to management about his making a personal call to his daughter in the Midwest without taking responsibility for the tab. She had listened in. Since he lacked an overcoat, the reporter headed south where he became famous with his own front-page column.)

I sat right down at my desk and proceeded to write the murder story, but George M. Currie, the Sunday editor, came over to beat me over the head verbally.

"I thought you would make a great reporter," he said. "But you left your post. How could you do such a thing?"

"Mr. Currie, we'll miss the edition," was all I could reply.

I told him I was "helping out" someone who was sick. Thompson was meantime writing the story back at the *Tribune* office with a combination of his and my facts. I was proud, exhausted and apprehensive of being fired from the *Eagle*. I think I was still making twenty-seven-fifty a week from the *Eagle*. The *Herald-Tribune*, shrine of all my dreams, paid me something like twelve dollars for my weekend work, and by this time, thanks to Sam Rubenstein, I made thirty-five dollars a week from Saint Joseph's College for Women as their public relations flack.

Because of Sam's blessed common sense, I've almost always had more than one job. I soon was able to pay half the rent at 150 Saint James Place, Brooklyn, where my parents and I and my grandmother, Nell Kennedy Toomey, wound up after my grandmother lost her brownstone at 75 Saint James Place because she was unable to pay the taxes. I also paid the phone bill, hired a cleaning lady, and opened a charge account at Bonwit Teller.

A CORRUPT ADMINISTRATION

In my idealism, pride and hauteur I accepted no gratuities and disliked those of the police who did. (Some didn't, of course, but many men were on the tab, and all plainclothesmen, I was firmly convinced.) During that administration, top police officials like Whalen were almost all notoriously on the take. A good-looking plainclothesman or vice cop once asked me out. In unladylike phrases I told my plainclothes admirer what I thought of plainclothesmen and he left the Shack, face burning, never to enter it again.

I didn't get fired from the *Eagle* but I did regretfully quit my *Herald-Tribune* job, turning it over to Robert Wacker. Bob and Ronnie Wacker are still dear friends, as well as among the few survivors of the *Eagle* staff with whom I'm still in touch. They also live on the east end of Long Island, on the North Fork on Nassau Point, Cutchogue, and are passionate conservationists as well as highly talented writers.

HAROLD, THE GOLDEN-TONGUED

Lunchtime, breakfast time, almost anytime was spent at one of the many bars in the neighborhood.

Because Harry ate there (though he no longer drank except for an occasional beer with Assistant District Attorney Turkus at Oetjen's, a Flatbush landmark), I frequented a place called the White Horse on Dean Street and Sixth Avenue, right down the street from the Shack. Etiquette required that the other beat men call their delinquent member if a big story broke while he was off drinking. Sam was too smart to hang out in bars and only attended if there was a testimonial dinner or benefit.

The bartender, Harold, weighed 350 pounds or more—and barely fit behind the bar. He was a masterful liar. If one of the *Daily News* printers from the Brooklyn plant down the street talked shop, Harold would interrupt to announce, "I wuz a printer down in Canarsie years ago. We put out them menus for Billy Ray's Bar."

Firemen learned that they were not alone in their heroic deeds. "When we lived in Queens, I wuz a volunteer with the Rosedale unit. We had that big brewery fire!" he would announce. The uniformed firefighters would stare incredulously at Harold's 300-pound-plus torso and shake their heads.

"Out Hicksville way I went along with the cops often," he was apt to announce when police were imbibing at his bar. "They needed me because I spoke the lingo of them hoods. I got some Eyetalian, you know."

To us would-be Hemingways, he had tried his hand at writing and had been on the staff of some obscure periodical like the *Police Gazette*.

"Didja know that back in Williamsburg, we had a paper, *The East River Bugle*, and I put it out for Joe Fiorello?" he once revealed to a dumbstruck audience of scribes.

To his boss, a morose individual with wizened features called "Flat Foot Willie Henderson," he was a subject of deep study, mixed with wonder.

"Willie," a Buster Keaton look-alike, rarely spoke, being more occupied with calculating his return. But one day, standing at the end of the bar wearing a pork-pie hat and looking more like Buster Keaton than ever, he made a short statement.

"Harold," he said, "the day youse tell these good people youse wuz ever a jockey is the day you're fired!"

One summer day, a truck with a block and tackle had to be summoned to lift Harold from behind the bar where he had overserved himself. His boss kept him on, however, since the episode helped business. Everyone was delighted with the spectcle of their bartender suspended in midair while the truck driver figured out how to lower him into the truck body. He recovered without further incident. He may have cut down on his intake, but never his lies.

AMNESIA CASE MYSTERY

True amnesia was a rarity. Usually cases reported to police involve elderly persons suffering from senile dementia. But one on the police blotter was different. An attractive brunette in her early twenties was found on Dean Street unconscious, after having jumped or been pushed out of a window.

"Plunged" was usually used to describe this ambiguous state. The only clue to her identity was a piece of paper found among her things when she was transferred from Kings County Hospital to the Bellevue psychiatric ward. The name on the scrap was "Anna Theriault" with an address on Visitation Place in Red Hook. I looked up Anna, bought her drinks, waited on the tenement steps for her to return from her nightly bar rounds and finally got her to accompany me and a photographer to Bellevue.

"Anna, I know a good bar right across from Bellevue. We'll go there after we see your friend!" I promised this tall, rangy alcoholic.

"OK!" she said.

Cameraman Al Lambert and I had to stop at the bar *before* the visit, though, to get her warmed up.

After several rounds I got her across to the hospital on the East River. Against a backdrop of parrot screams from those who had "eaten on the insane root that takes reason prisoner," Lambert, Anna and I went to visit the girl who was in bed, quiet but certainly not mad.

"This is where I'm going to wind up," groaned Lambert, a high-strung lensman not comfortable in a psycho ward.

"Take a few shots and get out of here," I advised him. "I'll grab the subway back."

I stayed, but tried to keep out of the way as the two young women chatted.

She finally told Anna that she was the daughter of the head of the Tuna Fishermen's Association in San Diego. I wired the anxious father at once. He flew into Kennedy, picked up his daughter at Bellevue and the girl was taken home to San Diego.

Anna had met her while both were patients in the Kings County psychiatric ward—Anna for alcoholism, the young woman for amnesia, real or simulated.

MISSING MILKMAN

Ed Potter was an obese and jovial Queens Assistant District Attorney who was a regular at political dinners. While he was on the dais one night, in evening clothes, an aide whispered to him that a nude man with a broken neck had turned up in a Forest Hills cellar. The death was classified as "suspicious."

Potter reluctantly left his dinner to report for duty. As he walked down the Queens street he noticed a milk wagon and horse, lacking a driver. Puzzled, he went to the cellar, examined the nude corpse, and then went through the building, asking tenants if they had any information. A young lady in a black lace nightgown seemed a little tipsy.

"Is your husband home?" Potter asked, gleam in eye, nose to windward.

"No, he works nights," she whispered.

"By any chance, were you entertaining the milkman tonight?"

"Yes," she admitted through her tears. "But he just vanished. I don't know what became of him. He got up to go to the bathroom and I ain't seen him since! I dunno where he went!" she kept saying, in between sobbing. "My husband will kill me if he ever finds out!"

"Never mind, Dear. I'll get to the bottom of this," Potter consoled her. And he did. Potter found that, instead of entering the bathroom door, the milkman had opened a dumb waiter and plunged four stories to his death. Potter gallantly promised to keep the incident a secret and did so, marking it "accidental death."

Potter, though stout, was fast on his feet. He chased me around his desk one day while I was trying to get some information from him. His wife and I had both attended the same Catholic boarding school, the Academy of Saint Joseph in Brentwood, Long Island.

"Ed, we Brentwood girls have a secret pact. We don't go to bed with other Academy girls' husbands," I said. It cooled him off.

Despite his goatish ways, Ed was the honored and presumably pious head of an annual Sunday school parade which was once a cherished tradition in Brooklyn and Queens.

Since I was out of the running, he took up with my favorite photographer, Phyllis Twachtman. They were an unlikely pair, the stout and merry lawyer and my skeletal friend who managed to drink herself to death at 48 by never eating.

My children loved "Aunt Phyllis." She kept an ice box full of Yoo-Hoo. Some were spiked, so she always warned them, "Don't drink Aunt Phyllis's Yoo-Hoo (which was filled with vodka), only the unopened cans!"

She died of cirrhosis on August 16th, 1969, a month after my father's death, also alcohol-related.

"Call Leo and tell him I'll be late," she instructed from her deathbed in Lenox Hill Hospital's intensive care unit. I pretended to dial WAtkins 9-6894, tears in my eyes, and talk to her longtime friend, an older man who really loved her and guided her in the investments market.

CUB'S DUTIES

Often I was delegated to go out by myself on minor stories to spare my older colleagues who, in turn, covered me and shared major stories with my inexperience. It was more than a fair deal.

This was what I was there for. I felt as though I belonged to a secret fraternity. I loved being outdoors, no matter what the weather.

On a freezing morning, three men were overcome in the hold of a ship at a Java Street pier in Greenpoint, Brooklyn. I took the subway out there and, as my mittens froze to the phone, called Harry first with the story before calling my own paper, the *Eagle*. I thawed out on the way back, stopping at a German bakery for hot coffee and buns.

Reporting early, seven o'clock in the morning, I had to check with someone about the night's activities. Besides reviewing the police slips across the street at the main desk, I trotted upstairs to Harry's office where the *Journal-American* reporter, Travis Fulton (nicknamed "Mission Bell") would be slumbering behind red velvet hangings on a cot with our mascot, the grey and white alley cat named Bum, on his chest.

"Anything happen overnight, Travis?"

"I have no idea!" he would say in all honesty. A descendant of Robert Fulton, inventor of the steamboat, Travis had an even more important asset. He had gone to school with one of the Hearsts! So drunk or sober, his job was safe.

A lovable gentleman no matter what his condition, Travis would leap to his feet, take off his hat, bow, and admit that he was completely unaware of what had gone on all night. Or he would share what he had. I would fill him in on any scraps of information gleaned from the cops across the street. Later, Travis came into his inheritance and retired to live as a gentleman farmer in Virginia. By that time he had given up drinking rather than scandalize the child of a WPIX reporter he married.

I saw him last one chilly night at the United Nations, covering Khrushchev.

"How are you, Jeanne, dear? You look lovely," this charming man said. Sober now, Travis looked every inch the gentleman he was.

"Please, take my coat," he typically insisted, draping his suit coat over my shoulders. He was, in truth, Chaucer's "verray parfit gentil knight."

EAST RIVER MAGIC

An incurable romantic, I loved the waterfront and read Ernest Poole's *The Harbor* with passionate recognition. The view from the Brooklyn Promenade of the shimmering towers of Manhattan was a favorite. I read a lot of Whitman (the *Eagle*'s most famous graduate) and sometimes took a room in a long-gone Brooklyn Heights hotel, the Tourraine, and wrote all night. Maybe someone would read my stories years after my death. Maybe, like Walt Whitman, I could call up a vision of the generations who would cross the East River after me, let those legions of river-crossers know that I, too, had heard the sea gulls cry, watched the flooding tide, the heartbreakingly beautiful sunrises and sunsets.

I haunted the longshoremen's halls, drank with the men, went out on small boats to see ships that had collided in the Narrows, and did many stories about exotic cargoes—giraffes, monkeys, tigers, and produce from all over the world—pineapples, coconuts, mangoes, saki and aquavit, even before I finally won the assignment.

Today I still turn sentimental when I hear the song, "I Cover the Waterfront," since I actually did it.

THE CRUX OF THE MATTER

During a Bethlehem Steel strike I was drinking with a gang of longshoremen in the back room of a waterfront bar near the Bush Terminal docks. A longshoreman's casual remark was a capsule explanation of how larceny crippled the Port of New York.

"Did you get any of those Italian cheeses that came in yesterday?" a burly dock worker asked his mate.

"No. The guard's looking pretty close at packages."

"I got one. I came through with a box. The guard made me open it. One of the dock cats jumped out and ran back to the pier.

"'I told you we've got mice at home and I'm taking home a cat! Now I have to go back for it,' I told him.

"'Oh! Go back and get your damned cat,' he muttered. So I ran back, grabbed a cheese, put it in the box, and sailed right through the gate!"

Minor though this incident was, it summed up the problem. Enormous losses led to the invention of the ship container which made some men like Jim Sherwood, who restored the Orient Express and put the world's most glamorous train back in service between London and Istanbul, immensely rich.

The Port of New York also lost business to Port Newark, Port Elizabeth and southern ports.

Though many of those who worked the docks were brigands, modern pirates, others were honorable perhaps because their successful careers removed them from the temptations faced by those at the bottom of the ladder, or perhaps they had a different standard of ethics.

I remember in particular Captain Phineas T. Blanchard of Turner and Blanchard, Stevedores. At a Sailors Snug Harbor benefit at the Downtown Athletic Club I cornered this sharp-eyed old salt and asked him for an interview.

"Blow, blow, blow the men down," he sang while reviewing my request handed to him on the dais in a scribbled note. "On condition that you take no notes at all," he decreed.

I was reviewing word association memory tricks as we rounded the end of West Street to the Battery.

In his hearty eighties, Captain Blanchard proceeded at a fast trot. In navy blue high- heeled pumps matching a conservative suit, my work uniform, I feared breaking an ankle as I struggled to keep up with him. Turner and Blanchard had handsome offices in a building facing the harbor, next to the Whitehall Building where my uncle, Captain William F. Toomey, presided as port captain for Gulf Oil.

Paintings of clipper ships on which Captain Blanchard had sailed adorned the reception area of his office. He got right into the interview. As he spun tales of sailing around the Horn on clipper ships, perilous storms off the Cape of Good Hope, exotic cargoes, and ports from Patagonia to China, I concentrated on memorizing the places, dates and events. My back was soaked. As soon as the interview ended, I went out to the hall and wrote down everything he said that I could remember.

Back in Brooklyn I bought a new blouse at a Montague Street shop and changed, throwing the sweat-soaked shirt in the garbage. I was a favored customer, often repairing there after covering a fire or other disaster to change clothes before reappearing at the office.

DANCING THE HORNPIPE

A few weeks later, Captain Blanchard was dancing the hornpipe for the young mariners on a splendid Norwegian school ship equipped with great sails, which visited the Port of New York from time to time.

The story about his career had appeared in "Harbor Lights," the waterfront column I did for years, the day after he had challenged my memory.

"She's a witch! Don't talk to her. Your every word will appear in her column," he laughingly warned his audience.

The nightside held me spellbound. On the streets at night, as families and individuals passed by going to movie theatres or restaurants in downtown Brooklyn, or just heading home to bed, I went by, often alone, sometimes with a photographer, to investigate a kidnapping or a murder or maybe just to do a feature story.

Brooklyn offered so much to a reporter with a roaming assignment. I was infatuated with the glamour of the waterfront: the blazing lights at night, the anchored foreign vessels in the Narrows, the bustling ferry boats and water taxis crossing the gleaming satiny river to Staten Island and the Jersey shore under a starlit sky.

I studied the ship bells and horns, all of which meant something, and wrote a listener's guide for the sleepless who heard the sounds at night.

Between the excitement of the City Room with its deadlines and working at Bergen Street and Manhattan Police Headquarters, my landing a newspaper job had turned out to be almost as good, maybe better than becoming a lawyer. It was certainly more fun. There were the police cars, emergency vehicles, handsome, uniformed police across the way, and enough murders, fires, explosions, even a double plane crash, plus a major jail break to keep me on the run.

SIGNAL 32 FOR 9 MEN

One freezing grey Brooklyn witner morning, the day after New Year's, I went across to the German bakery for a stollen and bought a bottle of red wine.

I was about to cut the stollen when the police radio cleared its throat, crackled and snapped, and then the dispatcher said, "Signal 32 for nine men— Ashland Place and DeKalb Avenue."

"The jail," I yelled, "the jail."

A few minute later, we were crammed in cabs on our way to the scene. It was so icy in the streets the men left their cars. Ashland Place and DeKalb Avenue was a down-at-the-heels, grey and shabby neighborhood near Fort Greene Park and the Brooklyn Navy Yard. The Raymond Street Jail, a Swiss cheese of jails, occupied an ancient grey stone building with turrets and iron bars, more ornamental than functional. Men were always breaking out.

The warden granted us a brief interview which revealed what we knew already. Nine men had escaped. Thousands of police were soon scouring the streets of Brooklyn and the other boroughs for them. We worked for days and nights at the scene, tracking down leads, interviewing police officials and the discomfited prison guards, whoever we could get to talk. As for the wine and stollen, I never saw either of them again.

A TIGHT SQUEEZE

All nine were ultimately recaptured.

Detective Nick Terranova, my future brother-in-law, took one in custody in a Hoboken bar. Another agile felon re-escaped, but only temporarily.

Bergen Street had sent an enormously fat detective out West to escort this man back, and the skinny rascal managed to get out the window of a men's room on the train. Dispatches from the Midwest city where he escaped reported that the obese sleuth had faithfully followed his charge's leap to freedom.

The *Detroit Free Press* news story described the detective's exit through the tiny window and a spirited chase down the tracks. I knew that had to be a lie. The detective could hardly make it through a normal door.

Some time after the jail break, Harry came out with an excellent exclusive story in the *New York World-Telegram*, an interview with a Corrections Department official with some interesting speculations. I caught hell from the *Eagle* for missing the story (though it was never offered, but reporters were supposed to have everything in their paper that the others carried).

I reproached Harry for not sharing it with me.

"I did it in my own time," was his answer.

Murder, Incorporated, by ADA Burton B. Turkus, was dedicated to Harry. Not only had he broken many exclusives about the gang of cutthroats who killed for money, usually insurance policies, but he came up with the bizarre nicknames like "Blue Jaw Magoon" which helped headline writers in their art of jazzing up murder. Harry named all our subjects including the hoods, murderers, cutthroats, villains, all who came our way, and all the hero dogs, cats up trees and other personalities of the police beat.

He was a master at humanizing beasts and was also blessed with a great love of justice. For this reason, Harry was often to be found at Saint Peter Claver's parish, an African-American parish in Bedford-Stuyvesant, working with the priests and the Urban League there. His example led me to take part, covering the Catholic labor meetings nights on my own time.

LOVE NEST RAID

Although I revered Harry, I was still competitive. Not long after his Raymond Street jail exclusive escape story, my late mother, a writer, poet and much loved wit, then employed by the Brooklyn DA's office, tipped me off on an exclusive.

In those innocent days, this involved a raid on the long-gone Bedford Hotel, rumored to be the favorite trysting place of half the illicit lovers in the borough.

The police acted on a now off-the-books or never-enforced morals law. Women wearing nothing under mink coats, high city officials and a number of middle-aged playboys were caught in this particular net and it created a front page exclusive byline story for me, complete with banner headline.

When I reported to work the next day, Harry was ruddy-faced. His cornflower blue eyes, a really extraordinary color I have never encountered since, were sending out electric blue radio signals. He was furious.

"What ingratitude! I've brought you up by hand, and you have the g-d audacity and gall to scoop me!"

"Harry," I told him, "I did it in my own time."

That was that. I had won my spurs and was now accepted as a full-fledged equal.

As a former law student, I asked Harry several times about making a will. He shuddered, said someone was walking over his grave and changed the subject. In 1948, while on vacation in Sarasota with Pete Terranova, I picked up the New York papers. I was reading the obit of Richard K. Lauterbach, author of *Danger from the East*, predicting the Communist takeover of China, when my eye strayed down the page and caught a smaller head: "H. T. Feeney Rites Are Held." I broke down and cried. Pete finally asked if Harry and I had been lovers.

"No. Like Sam, he was my teacher. Whatever I learned about covering news, he and others at Bergen Street taught me," I explained through my sobs. It was like losing a beloved uncle. As I had feared, Harry died intestate, just five years after we had had our conversation on wills. His affairs were left a mess, causing great anguish to his second wife and family. But in my many years of working with other newsmen, Harry T. Feeney stands out as one of the greatest legmen (or non-writing reporters) I ever met. I still remember with a smile his impatience with the occasional dolt who dropped by to ask him to run something in the *New York World-Telegram* or *New York Daily Mirror*, both long since consigned to newspaper limbo.

"Is this the story of your life?" he would ask. Or, "Could you boil that down to a paragraph?" Or, "When do you go to press?"

Though I really didn't have any faith in astrology, I found it a strange coincidence that Sam, Harry and I were all born under the sign of Leo. We used to have a big birthday party for ourselves every August.

A knock at the door came one August day while I was cutting the collective birthday cake. "Find out who's there!" Harry was playing poker with Jesse Strait, a *New York Daily Mirror* cameraman, and a couple of other men.

"It's Joe Kiernan," I reported. Kiernan, a good-looking silver-haired Irishman, was well liked but he worked under Mike O'Brien, which meant he was cut out of any top stories we could manage to keep from him.

"Give him a piece of cake. Don't let him in," ordered Harry.

Letting the *World-Telegram* office door shut in poor Kiernan's face, I went for a slice of cake. When I returned, I handed him the cake and quietly closed the door again, leaving him in the hallway.

The *News* office was, like Harry's, on the second floor of our ramshackle headquarters but separated by a small, dusty landing and a few steps, putting it in another wing of the ancient wooden apartment building. A poker game sometimes went on between calls checking out details on a hot story.

NEWS OF ANIMALS

Sometimes things were slow and it was possible to just walk around the mean streets, soak up atmosphere and occasionally come across animal features. My passion for animals ultimately brought me to Connecticut as head of The Last Post, an animal Club Med in Falls Village.

I had an affinity for stories about cats up trees, neglected dogs, mounted men's horses and other creatures, including a snowy owl who somehow made its way from Alaska to Floyd Bennett Field.

Harry made sure that all animals had names and if none was reported, he invented one. His brother, Charley Feeney, was the undoubted champion of "piping," or jazzing a story up by finding an angle—ghost stories for Halloween, kind actions by individuals or neighborhoods at Christmas, a mother and adult child reunited on Mother's Day, and so on.

Though Charley Feeney was the acknowledged champion at embellishing stories with a little fiction, pipe artists existed elsewhere. A cynical lensman in Philadelphia always carried a doll which would appear often in fire pictures, seemingly accidentally dropped in the street or in a burned-out building, poignant relic of a hopefully rescued child. It was his prop kept in the trunk of his car.

COURTS OF JUSTICE

Trials were a favorite assignment, perhaps tinged with regret that I was in the press box and not beside the defendant as defense counsel, or opposing him as prosecutor.

The Benjamin Feldman case involved the murder of Feldman's wife and his mother-in-law, Gussie Berkowitz, with enough strychnine to kill twenty horses. During the trial it turned out that a third person had also been murdered: Feldman's unborn son. The brilliant Hyman Barshay, though he won for the defense, pushed his grateful client away after winning his freedom. Feldman later relocated to Mexico City where some unsuspecting señorita married him.

Observing legal virtuosity was a major part of covering courts. County Court Judge Samuel Leibowitz was a master of getting criminals off as a defense lawyer and one of the most severe in handing out long sentences or execution after he became a judge in the Kings County Court. He correctly predicted the future criminal career of Carmine "The Snake" Persico, brought before him on some minor charge while still a teen-ager.

PROBE OF BEDFORD-STUYVESANT

With then-District Attorney Miles F. McDonald, Judge Leibowitz launched a sweeping Grand Jury probe of the Bedford-Stuyvesant section, the main African-

American section of Brooklyn. Eleanor Roosevelt came to the defense of the Bed-Stuy residents, most of whom were honest, hard-working men and women. She was often the main attraction at meetings held in churches throughout the area, usually at night, and I covered those meetings.

She was a vibrant woman, intellectually alive, and a marvelous speaker, detested by the right. She was also my friend, Virginia's heroine.

"Here's a press card," I said one warm evening. "I'm covering the First Lady at an AME church in Bedford-Stuyvesant. Why not come to hear her? I know how much you admire her."

Virginia and I had become lifelong friends as children in the fourth grade at the Academy of Saint Joseph in Brentwood, Long Island, then a boarding school. Our mothers were also long-lost childhood friends. They rediscovered each other in the parlors of Brentwood one Sunday.

That night, after hearing Mrs. Roosevelt's address, Virginia asked, "Who was that blond man at the end of the press table?"

"Johnny Deraval," I replied. "Why? Are you interested?"

The next afternoon I brought John, who then worked for the long-gone Standard News Association, later the *New York World-Telegram*, over to the house at 134 Lafayette Avenue (where I was a non-paying guest) to introduce him, and in six months' time they were married. I was maid of honor as she was to be my matron of honor when Peter Terranova and I made it legal.

I saw Mrs. Roosevelt again at the next Christmas party of the Newswomen's Club of New York. Her syndicated column, "My Day," qualified her for membership. I have been a member for more than fifty years. Eleanor Roosevelt came to our parties and always insisted that the media send women reporters to her interviews, thereby helping the cause of female acceptance in the news field.

She detested alcohol, and I still remember the First Lady's reserved expression at that Christmas party.

Mrs. Roosevelt wore a high-necked black bombazine dress and sat in a rocking chair. The attractive blond dynamo Jean Dalrymple, then head of the City Center, sat in a kittenish way on the floor, exposing her considerable decolletage. She was by no means drunk, but like most party-goers had enjoyed a few Christmas toddies.

Though always gracious, the First Lady seemed a trifle turned off by the jokes and general uproar. Pulling over a straight chair, Edith Barber, food editor of the long-gone *New York Sun* and our hostess, settled herself beside our famous guest.

"I have been anxious to talk to you personally, and tell you how thrilled we are that you joined us," she said. "We're all so grateful for your loyalty. Having women assigned to your press conferences means a lot to all of us."

Mrs. Roosevelt smiled and seemed happy to be back on a serious topic.

HARBOR LIGHTS

My final *Eagle* assignment, ship news, came about because of my very obvious preoccupation with everything maritime: distant ports, exotic cargoes and eccentric seafarers. I also had some great maritime contacts through my father's brother, Captain William F. Toomey, who had been the youngest captain in the Merchant Marine in the First World War. Torpedoed three times, he yet saved everyone.

When he returned to the family brownstone in Brooklyn, my grandfather, John Toomey, asked, "Did you pray when you were in the water, Son?"

"Yes, Father. I did."

"What was your prayer?"

"I wish to Christ I could get these damned boots off."

In 1951, I was named ship news editor of the *Brooklyn Daily Eagle*, a category that no longer exists.

Nowadays, even the average traveler flies back and forth to distant locations like a migrating bird. Then, reporters made the six a.m. cutter daily and sailed out to the Narrows to board the great ships coming in from Europe. The Coast Guard cutter carried pilots, customs men, Immigration and Naturalization officials as well as the press. We all drank Coast Guard coffee and rode the waves and swells in foul weather as well as fine, in dense fogs, snow and rain.

We interviewed the rich, the famous, and sometimes the infamous aboard as a ship went up the North River, attended by a gaggle of tug boats, to her berth. Special events, like the triumphant return of the S.S. *United States* to the Port of New York after breaking the world record by crossing the Atlantic in three days, ten hours, were greeted by geysers of water from celebrating fireboats.

The United States Line, the American Export Line, the French Line, the Italian Line and Cunard were the major passenger lines. Moore-McCormack, the Farrell Line and other freighters could take passengers if they kept the number to under twelve. Carrying more than twelve passengers required that a doctor be aboard.

A VISTA OF STACKS

It was thrilling to view the majestic steamships from a nearby office building or overhead from a plane, lying in their berths in a neat parallel row on the North River before setting out on voyages to distant places. By deducting 40 from the pier number, you could learn the street. For instance, Pier 90 would be found at the foot of Fiftieth Street and for all I know, it still is!

I memorized what the whistles meant: docking, departing, passing another vessel, to starboard or to port, or simply letting everyone know that the ship had arrived in the spectacular Port of New York.

To be young with good health, an active constitution, a sense of adventure and to have that assignment was a kind of heaven.

Being abroad at dawn with Shakespeare's heavenly alchemy, "gilding pale streams," suffusing the eastern sky, setting the windows of the skyscrapers ablaze as Paul Verlaine once described the fiery glitter in Paris, with the invigorating scent of salt water and tar, was intoxicating.

I made the six a.m. Coast Guard cutter every weekday morning to board the great ships coming in from Europe. I never once missed it. An AP photographer named Tony Camareno would usually follow me, holding my skirt together as well as carrying his camera.

"I'm amazed you're still alive," a tugboat captain once greeted me. "I saw you go up so many ladders with the ship rising and falling with the tide that I thought sure you'd fall in."

SHIPBOARD INTERVIEWS

Personalities in the news were our assignment. Among those I interviewed were Winston Churchill, the Archbishop of Canterbury, the golfer Ben Hogan, the actors Alan Ladd and Charles Boyer, and my hero, Fairfield Osborne, head of the

New York Zoological Society.

There were also brutal stories out of the waterfront beat. Murders, hijackings, assaults and long drawn-out labor disputes between the shippers and the International Longshoremen's Association also made the headlines. City editor Hank Connors christened the column "Harbor Lights." I still get nostalgic, missing the salt spray, the tides rising and falling, the bustle of the docks, whenever I hear the song "Harbor Lights."

The ship news reporters were an interesting and hearty band. An observing spectator would have been able to pick them out from their colleagues. One thing they all had in common was a ruddy complexion, a healthy glow, since they were outdoors every day instead of being cooped up in a smoke-filled City Room. Sometimes the reddish tint was aided by alcohol which was available to us in all the press rooms aboard the vessels entering the Port of New York.

George Horne was top ship news man for the *Times*, Walter Hamshar was ship news editor of the *Herald-Tribune*, and Jim Duffy of the *World-Telegram* was dean of New York ship news reporters. I was the only woman ship news editor in New York, though a capable woman handled ship news for the Port of Baltimore.

UNION BOSS VANISHES

A major exclusive came about by chance. I was working in the *Eagle* City Room one afternoon when Johnny, our aged male receptionist, reported that a "Mrs. Flaherty" wanted to see me.

The elderly "boy," or receptionist, was a sixty-five-year-old white man, short and round, with no news judgment at all which is why he was still a "copy boy" despite his years.

Generally, the "hall cases" he admitted to the City Room were worthless from a news viewpoint: outright lunatics, drunks, prostitutes or other hopeless and hapless flotsam and jetsam of any great city.

One believed he was king of the Micronesian Islands, another was eternally trying to persuade the paper to do an exposé on the bacteria which he was convinced covered the dishes and plates of *all* Fulton Street establishments from the austere Gage and Tollner's where the judges (and I, when I had the price) dined, to the humblest Nedick's.

A perturbed woman was receiving unwanted radio signals via her poor brain from Russia, and so on. Thus, it was no great treat to be told that anyone wanted to see me in the hall.

A thin, handsome Irish woman, mother of seven, hardworking and devout, proved the exception. She arrived one afternoon to report her husband, John, missing. Mrs. Flaherty handed me my first major exclusive since the hotel raid.

"He was due home Friday night," she related, "but he never came home. We haven't heard a word and he never called."

"Was he worried about anything?" I asked her gently.

"There were some union problems," she acknowledged. "He was with the Grain Handlers. They wanted to break away from the ILA."

Missing people were nothing new. Most had left for compelling reasons: harried by bill collectors, strong-arm men, sometimes involved in impossible romantic and sexual entanglements. A few turned up in the river, suicides, and there were an infinitesimal number who represented an element of mystery.

STRUGGLE ON THE DOCKS

John Flaherty was in this rare category and the story was promising because he happened to be a longshoreman, head of the Grain Handlers Union, a somewhat feisty ILA (International Longshoremen's Association) branch.

I thought it completely possible that Flaherty had been murdered.

No one knows what really happened to John Flaherty. He had some enemies. But he was also a heavy drinker and might have simply tumbled into Gowanus Canal, Brooklyn's "Lavender Lake," from which his partially decomposed body was hauled two months after his disappearance.

AN EXCLUSIVE

Waterfront violence has been brilliantly and accurately portrayed in Budd Schulberg's *On the Waterfront*. Whatever the truth, I had gotten a major exclusive.

The New York papers picked up the story from the *Eagle* and I was being praised by the editors, a heady feeling.

"Would you run a picture of John?" the troubled wife had asked me. I was happy to do so. We ran it with a moody night shot of Sackett Street, a line of brooding houses, and the lighted corner saloon where the missing man was last seen.

The following day we featured a photo of Mrs. Flaherty and her seven children waiting for news. Flaherty had walked out of that waterfront bar into oblivion.

"She's one of our own," I heard a relative whisper. Being an Irish-American was an asset on the docks.

To me, as a young reporter, the case had everything: mystery, a Victorian setting with a waterfront saloon, fog horns—right out of Eugene O'Neill. The tin ceiling was decorated with fleur de lis and there was a century-old mahogany bar with antique brass spittoons. In the way of writers, we often called these objects of disgusting use gaboons, so obscure a term that I never heard it again. Yet the erudite Wilkinson insisted that was a medieval term for cuspidors.

Burly dock workers lined the bar. The bartender looked astonished and none too pleased to find a woman reporter belting boilermakers with the best of them.

The most exciting, magical part of all this was the waterfront itself, that vast busy corridor to the Atlantic which made the Port of New York the greatest harbor in the world. Another ingredient back in the 1940s was youth, which made the whole gleaming expanse of shining water, the soaring towers of New York, the busy tugs, lighters, tow boats, the ferry boats, blazing with lights, a vision of hope and excitement.

I begged for and obtained permission to drop everything and concentrate on "The Strange Disappearance of John Flaherty," as we headlined the story.

Since Flaherty had been last seen at that Sackett Street waterfront bar the night he vanished, it remained our only lead. I returned many times with a cameraman, launching my visits (and boilermaker consumption) the same night Mrs. Flaherty had poured her story into my ear.

"When did you see him last?" I asked the bartender.

"Eight o'clock, the night he disappeared," was the answer.

No one at the bar seemed to be able to add anything to that.

DEFYING THE ILA

But later, one of the men who was there that night phoned me to say, "He was planning a new union, the Grain Handlers, to be separate from the ILA." The bosses were not happy.

The bartender said he was not drunk, but mindful of the ABC regulations. (That was always the claim, even if someone had to be carried out of a place.)

I set out daily, talking to longshoremen and to detectives Clarence Gilroy and his partner, John McGuire of the 76th, the Hamilton Avenue squad in Red Hook, a waterfront Brooklyn neighborhood of century-old fascinating houses and ILA halls.

FROZEN IN TIME

There were pockets like this throughout New York, neighborhoods where time stood still. You might come upon a barber shop with personalized shaving mugs used by famly members for generations, International Longshoremen's Association halls heated by coal-burning belly stoves, old-time saloons with beveled glass mirrors, mahogany bars. Flaherty's last stop was such a scene.

The missing dock leader finally did turn up in Gowanus Canal and three men were indicted for his murder. Lack of evidence caused eventual dismissal of the charges. After viewing the remains, I went back to the *Eagle*. The corpse had been a frightful sight, blackened, with eels coming out from various body apertures.

I was calmly eating a frozen custard when I got back to the *Eagle*. The desk men branded me the "resident ghoul," and the editors were satisfied that I was qualified to cover Bergen Street.

ROMANTIC, OR MAYBE NOT

The love life of the Fourth Estate was then, and probably still is, a subject full of laughter, not passion. My colleagues at Bergen Street (and I, too) put an exclusive first on our list of priorities.

This is not to say that many were not contentedly married. But among the single reporters, which included myself, love was less than passing. It was almost negligible. Casual sex was the usual thing.

Manny, Sam Rubenstein's and my dayside office mate, seemed bent on seducing all the women in the neighborhood, including a nymphomaniac school teacher who would go berserk when drinking and then, sober if hung over, next day would pass us all by at the Reporters' Shack without a word or a glance after having been Mata Hari the night before.

Manny seemed about to add to his list of conquests a young, rather ill-favored Italian-American girl named Aggie, who worked in the underwear factory down the street. One day I heard from a Major Crimes Unit detective that Aggie was closely related to a mob figure who lived on Carroll Street near Nick Monte's Venetian Gardens Restaurant in South Brooklyn.

The next day when the Don Juan of the Fourth Estate showed up in our tiny office, I gave him a cold glance and said, "Woodsman, spare that tree!"

"What's wrong with you, Toomey?" he inquired.

When I filled him in on Aggie's antecedents and relations he suddenly became very chilly in manner to the poor girl, who stopped dropping in to gossip with me and flirt with the attractive Manny. It was this same lovable philanderer who showed me my first "Wire Room," a block or so from police headquarters, and clued me in on the fact that many of our uniformed companions were well aware of the existence of the betting parlor and paid to ignore it.

EAGLE WINS THE PULITZER

Ed Reid of the *Eagle* in 1951 won the paper the Pulitzer for his exposé of police corruption, based on a conversation he overheard in The Eagle's Nest, a bar across the street from the *Eagle* in Joe's Restaurant. The series he wrote resulted in indictments, suicides and some convictions. The police beat reporters usually were not assigned to corruption investigations, perhaps because becoming the enemy would cut them off from information. They were rarely assigned to exposés.

City desks usually assigned staff hatchet men to cover internal affairs probes or grand jury investigations of police corruption.

Reid's exposé was like a Bureau of Internal Affairs probe, suddenly revealing what everyone close to the police knew already but did nothing about.

In Brooklyn, venal officers were paid off by the bookie, Harry Gross, in the Dugout, a bar near Ebbets Field then called home by "Dem Bums," the Brooklyn Dodgers, who later deserted us for Los Angeles.

MANY-COLORED RADIANCE

A gorgeous stained glass window in Joe's Bar portrayed a large eagle atop a nest of twigs. The legend "The Eagle's Nest" was engraved in lead under the bird's talons.

While on the *New York Journal-American* I wrote a sentimental column about that bar and all the long-gone *Eagle* scribes whose faces once shone in the many-colored light from the prismatic giant window: Harold Burr, a sports writer; Jane Corby, *Eagle* motion picture critic; Helen Worth, lovelorn columnist; Sunday editor George Currie; court reporters Freddy Anderson and Wendell Hamner, and political editor Joe Schmalacker were just a few I mentioned.

When home in Southampton I often covered the regular pretty dull beats for various weeklies, including board of education meetings in Pierson High School in Sag Harbor.

Dr. John Bishop, a longtime Sag Harbor Board of Education president, laughingly informed me years later that one time I stood up and recited a Shelley couplet:

> Life, like a dome of many-colored glass,
> Stains the bright radiance of Eternity

at an otherwise normal meeting. Mortified, also surprised, I made a much overdue apology. My drinking often led to behavior which puzzled everyone, even me.

But I must have been reflecting on that stained glass window.

U.S. NAVY GROUPIE

The body of an attractive dark-haired woman was found in the rhododendron bushes of the American Museum of Natural History one summer evening. She had been strangled. The police issued pictures of the lady and revealed that while her husband, a traveling salesman, was on the road, she reportedly dated sailors. Since the fleet was in, they suspected a sailor might be the murderer.

With the famed photographer Charley Hough, whose prizewinning photo of the burrning of the German zeppelin Hindenburg at her mooring in Lakehurst, New Jersey on May 6, 1937, was a classic, I set out on a West Side barhopping expedition.

"Have you seen this lady in here lately?" Charley or I would ask the bartender, showing him our picture obtained from the police.

Of course we had to order a round, sometimes drinks for several customers, while playing detective. Though we hoped to discover the murderer's identity, all that happened was that I got drunk.

I came to in a *New York Daily News* parking lot as Charley developed his photos. He then drove me home to Brooklyn. Next morning I woke up with a major hangover and an even greater fear.

Had I called in the story?

I ran down three stories and retrieved the Sunday *Eagle*, which was delivered.

"Woman Strangled on Museum Grounds" was the lead headline on Page One. My byline appeared below. I was saved. I had phoned in the story before passing out.

The murder was never solved and I never tried that method of reporting again.

THE NAKED TRUTH

The photographers to a man seemed determined to get every woman to take off her clothes and pose naked for them. (Not me, I was one of the gang and wise to them.)

It was extraordinary how susceptible to flattery many women were. Once I learned what the lensmen were up to, I was careful about intruding on them. Police news photographers were apt to be filming vain and susceptible maidens and matrons almost anywhere. (But they really came into their own covering ship news.)

Coming into the *Eagle* one day, I missed my pretty friend Shirley Krasnoff. She used to come Fridays to grab my paycheck from me for my share of the rent before I squandered it.

"Have you seen my friend Shirley?" I asked the receptionist.

"She went off towards the photo studio with one of the photographers," he said.

I found her in the photo studio. One of the lensmen had somehow gotten her to pose for him in the buff.

"Give me all the negatives or I'll get your neck," I warned him. I think I got back all the negatives plus a positive or two. Unretouched, they looked very clinical.

FRIED TROLLOPS

Police reporters were a colorful lot. Joey George of the *News* got banned from the Elks Club after shooting up their chandelier; "Stitch" McCarthy, another *News* man, reportedly was cut off at the Waldorf-Astoria after wrestling with the furniture; and a Mr. Malaprop, named Bart Paganini of the *World-Telegram*, tried to rewrite the language.

Recovering from a hangover, he called for "fried trollops" at the local fish restaurant, the Triangle, at the junction of Flatbush Avenue, Sixth Avenue and Bergen Street. Phoning in the details of an accident, he said, "The injured woman is in a comma—no, a kimono."

Calling up a woman whose husband had just fallen from a skyscraper under construction, Bart asked, "Was your husband wearing a truss?" And, "Does he have false teeth?"

The mystified matron naturally asked why he was asking.

"Well," said Bart, "I think he may have slipped and fell on the job."

Another time, checking another fatality, he asked the victim's wife, "Is this the Widow Brown?"

Paganini had one big asset though. He spoke Italian. He was able to beat us all when the case involved Italians.

Wacker, who followed me to Bergen Street, was and still is an inveterate wag... In filling him in about his new assignment, I told him to be sure to wake up the *News* night reporter Joey George when he came in mornings, because Mike O'Brien, boss of the *News* Brooklyn bureau, was always threatening to get him fired if he got drunk or even seemed hungover.

"'Wake up! Mike O'Brien is coming!' is all you have to yell, and he'll be on his way," I told Bob.

One morning Bob saw Joey asleep, as usual, in the old one-armed lounge chair in the *Eagle* office. Beside him on the armrest were his false teeth. Having just had a wisdom tooth extracted, Bob placed his molar beside the plate and yelled, "Wake up! Mike O'Brien is coming!"

Leaping to his feet, Joey threw the plate into his mouth, spotted an extra, and went out the door trying to fit it into his plate.

VICTORIAN SPLENDOR

The Manhattan Shack at Four Centre Market Place was directly behind the baroque Victorian headquarters building at 240 Center Street, where Teddy Roosevelt was once Commissioner. It is now an expensive residential property.

When Pete Terranova, my second husband, was a patrolman, often considered the best-looking and best-dressed cop in New York, he was assigned as combination secretary and watchdog at a desk just outside of Police Commissioner Lewis Valentine's office, which included a rococo portico over Broome Street.

Police stations, like newspapers, attract lunatics. Fanatics, possessed by delusions and obsessions, gravitated to police headquarters to relay news that Russia was sending them radio signals, or to tell Valentine how to run the city's police force.

Pete would push a button hidden under his desk.

In a few minutes a cop, attired in a white coat, would enter the office and proceed to scrutinize the visitor, while taking notes. A few seconds and the lunatic would leave the office, sprint down the marble stairs and take off, convinced that the cop was a psychiatrist about to send him back to Bellevue and a locked ward.

JULIUS CAESAR AT BAT!

As time went on, newspapers and the wire services hired college graduates but properly kept the old district men, most of whom were very able reporters, on the payroll by a kind of grandfather's clause. Much of the color of the newspaper business disappeared as the old reporters gradually were replaced by "school of journalism" grads.

Many of my co-workers were strictly legmen or district men, who phoned in their stories and were not writers. Some were almost illiterate. Mike Finnegan of the *New York World-Telegram* was a faithful and decent reporter, but he had no formal education. A rewriteman once mentioned Julius Caesar to Mike, who was phoning in a story.

"Who was this guy Julius Caesar?" Mike asked his colleagues on the Manhattan police beat.

"He played shortstop for the Cincinnati Reds," some comedian yelled back, and Mike offered this crumb of information to his rewriteman.

WHERE'S JOHNNY SHINE?

The AP phone rang constantly in the hall. As a cub, I was expected to answer this. Saturday night the caller was often Herman Appleman of the *New York Journal-American* where I wound up later.

"Put Shine on the phone," Appy would say.

Though Johnny Shine was a grand fellow, he had a big thirst.

"Mr. Shine is at the Safe and Loft squad," I might lie. Then I would importantly dial whatever number Shine had entrusted to me.

One place answered, "Mike's Corned Beef and Cabbage House." A stunned silence followed my request for the missing reporter. "I haven't seen him for weeks," a nasal voice informed me.

Appy kept calling and I kept making excuses.

Shine, when sober, was a remarkable reporter. He never took a note and never made a mistake, even when covering a detailed court story.

When Appy seemed overly excited, I would usually fill him in on whatever was going on, as I was to do later on for Al Turk when a big court story broke in Brooklyn.

I got Turk out of the bar OK, but he was just too drunk to make any sense. I climbed into the phone booth and interrupted him, telling the rewriteman, "Mr. Turk has a terrible cold. This is Jeanne Toomey of the *Journal*. Do you mind if I fill in for him?"

"No, go ahead. I noticed," said the rewriteman, who also kept his mouth shut and did not turn Turk in. This was a kind of gentleman's agreement, to cover a fellow reporter taken drunk. It was not like sharing an exclusive, which was a different thing.

FOUNDING THE PRESS CLUB

To improve relations between cops, district attorneys, and the Fourth Estate, in 1948 a gaggle of us decided to start a press club.

Meeting at the Martinique, then a middle-class residential hotel at Herald Square in Manhattan, but for decades since a welfare hotel, we set it up. Initially, we called it The Newspaper Reporters Association. Later, when electronic media took over, it became simply The New York Press Club, which in 1998 observed a fiftieth anniversary. We met periodically down the hall from the Bell Club, made up of fire department buffs and groupies.

But we shone brightest with our Christmas parties, still a regular function. In keeping with modern times, the liquor intake nowadays seems way down. Reporters then did more elbow bending than dancing.

After many drinks, Willie Keegan of the *New York Post* was apt to ask: "Do you see any green in these eyes?"

His eyes had always turned bright emerald, which, in his case, was the reverse of traffic signals, meaning STOP!

Justice Charles Ramsgate of the Special Sessions Court once drove an inebriated lady back to her Park Avenue residence from one of our events, with me along as chaperone. We got her into her apartment and into bed. The entrance door opened right into the bedroom.

His Honor was very happy that I was along when, after hearing him say that he had always wanted to see a lady in black underwear, the pretty matron stripped to bra and panties which indeed were black. I had just gotten her tucked in when the door abruptly opened and her husband strode in.

"Hi!" I greeted him. "We were just leaving."

PARTY-LOVING BOSS

On the *Eagle*, the city editor was Edwin Whitmore Wilkinson, a wealthy man in his own right. His family owned many apartment buildings in Brooklyn's Bedford Stuyvesant section and some office property, including a building on Livingston Street where Red Cross Shoes was a tenant. In our feckless youth the idea that anyone had independent wealth was so rare as to be nearly unbelievable.

Wilkinson always bought at Sonsire's, the bar across the street from the *Eagle*, and no one argued with him since we knew he was rich and we were not.

His posture of buying the drinks made him also the arbiter of when the drinking was to commence. Every afternoon, near quitting time, watched by a score of thirsty reporters, Wilkinson would head for the men's room. Half German, half Welsh by descent, he was a fanatic about cleanliness. Male writers reported with awe that he all but took a bath in the men's room sink, scrubbing up to his shoulders as though ready to commence surgery. Then, glowing, his cheeks rosy, he would return to the City Room to summon the waiting hordes of impecunious scribes.

His "Will you join me?" summons was greeted by a mad rush to the elevator by the older employees, to the fire stairs by the youths and youthesses. (Young female reporters were dubbed "youthess" by John Rogan of the *Mirror*, and it stuck.)

A STORY NEVER TOLD

One warm afternoon, as thoughts of gin coolers danced in my head, a plump lady from Brighton Beach arrived as a "hall case." The imbecilic receptionist asked Wilkinson who could see her.

Since I was the top expert on "the rising handshake," a method of getting hall cases in and out of the building with speed, Wilkinson designated me to hear the woman's story.

What her story was I don't know. I do know that her name was Mrs. Sarah Cohen and that her problem seemed endless.

The hour was approaching five, and Wilkinson's troops were rapidly putting away notebooks and pens, closing desks, making fast visits to the lavatories and, in short, getting ready for a fast exodus to the main event—getting drunk at Sonsire's on Wilkinson.

Since he liked all the troops to leave at once, he kept glancing my way in exasperation.

Finally, rising to his lanky six feet-plus, he came over, introduced himself graciously, and said, "May I invite you, Mrs. Cohen, to join us in a libation or two over at a modest establishment across the street?"

The good woman smiled assent and seemed under the impression that we were about to feed her.

In deference to her age and weight, I took the elevator with her and saw her into Sonsire's. Once caught up in the spirit of revelry that prevailed there, I forgot all about her.

The juke box played tunes of the forties—"Don't Sit Under the Apple Tree," "I'll Walk Alone," Chattanooga Choo Choo," and even older songs like "Those Wedding Bells Are Breaking Up that Old Gang of Mine," and we all sang along. A favorite maudlin number was "You Tell Me Your Dreams, and I-I-I-I [dragged out] Will Tell You Mine!"

Sonsire's, Joe's, where we ate when we had the price, and the Hole in the Wall are all gone now, replaced by Memorial Plaza. The "new" Supreme Court building stands where the *Eagle* irregulars once ground out Brooklyn's only daily at Johnson and Fulton Streets.

On that summer day in the forties at Sonsire's, I at last stopped singing along and took a look at Mrs. Cohen. The poor woman looked totally different. Her wisps of grey hair were now plastered over her forehead. Her eyes seemed glazed and she was holding onto the pine bar as though crossing the Alps in a blizzard.

"Hey, Wilkie, look what you've done!" I called over to my boss (and sometimes casual boyfriend).

"Ye gods!" he said. "Jeanne, come here and give me a hand."

The two of us managed to get her out to the street. When the fresh air (as fresh as Brooklyn provided) hit her, she reeled. I shuddered.

Wilkinson, who could hold more liquor and stay on his feet than anyone else on the paper, summoned a taxi.

Putting his foot on the door ledge, he said, "Driver! I am Edwin Whitmore Wilkinson, city editor of the *Brooklyn Daily Eagle*. This is Mrs. Cohen."

In an aside, he extracted her address from the poor sodden creature. "I want you to take Mrs. Cohen to this address and see her into her apartment in Brighton Beach. If anything goes amiss, it will go hardly with you. I have your name and hack number."

He then handed the appalled driver a bill of larger denomination than the man had ever seen in the area. We went back into the bar. We never heard from Mrs. Cohen again.

BANNED

Parties were frequent and wild as a brush fire. When Managing Editor Robert M. Grannis announced his forthcoming departure to the *Pittsburgh Post-Gazette*, the women's department, of which I was relieved and grateful *not* to be a member, arranged the farewell brawl.

Their first mistake was to book us into the prim and staid Towers Hotel, much favored by wealthy widows. Only cocktails were served, another mistake.

It was a hot day in August and the intoxication was rapid, general and lethal.

Staggering out, I was with (now, alas, departed) Irene Neer, soon to become the wife of a foremost freelance writer, Lester David (since deceased) and Veronica Winifred Ann Halkenhauser, a gorgeous blond (later Mrs. Robert Wacker and the mother of five handsome blond sons including my godson, Chris Wacker).

Since Ronnie lived way uptown, near the Bronx, we thought it best for her to stay overnight with me. I was still living then with my best friend Virginia Henschel, the same one who directed me to apply at the *Eagle*, the dear girl with whom I had gone to boarding school, and her family at 134 Lafayette Avenue in downtown Brooklyn, a few blocks from the Academy of Music and, even more important, a few blocks from Bergen Street.

Al Leiner, a police reporter, carried Ronnie and we all got into a taxi. Some elderly, grey-haired man, ancient to us (he must have been at least forty-five) was running alongside the taxi yelling, "Ronnie! Miss Halkenhauser!"

CHASING AN AD MAN

"Begone, you masher. You should be ashamed at your age," I yelled out the window at the man who I found out later was Ronnie's former boss at an advertising agency in New York, and her invited escort at the party!

Once at my friend's family-owned brownstone, Leiner carried Ronnie up three flights of stairs and placed her tenderly on my bed. Though unconscious, she kept modestly pulling her skirt down as she was carried upstairs.

The men left. Irene and I, in our slips, tiptoed down to the basement or ground floor which, as in all standard brownstones, contained the kitchen. We phoned Ronnie's mother in upper Manhattan to tell her that her daughter was staying overnight with me, having caught a bad cold.

As we opened the refrigerator, looking for something cold to drink, there was a noise at the basement door.

Both of us leaped into a closet in a dining room which was sometimes converted to a bedroom. Due to the war and the proximity of the house to the Brooklyn Navy Yard, the Henschel family occasionally rented out rooms to sailors.

I heard Virginia's mother, Molly Henschel, say, "Now this room is large, near the entrance. The bathroom is one flight up and you can have kitchen privileges."

We held our breaths, difficult since we were almost on top of a huge, dusty vacuum cleaner.

"And there's plenty of closet space," she went on. I felt a trickle of sweat go down my back. Now she would surely open the door, revealing us in our intoxicated condition in our underwear.

But fate was with us. The voices became distant and faded out. All was silence. In about ten minutes the two of us left the closet and went upstairs to go to bed in other bedrooms in the four-story high brownstone.

UNDER THE TABLE

Irene (who died of a cerebral hemorrhage in 1995) was assigned to sleep in Virginia's brother's room. He was a captain in the Air Force and at the time, a prisoner of war in Germany. It took several Alka-Seltzers next morning for me to make it to Bergen Street, and the other two didn't feel any better.

Also, the Towers banned us from ever having a party there again. We had forgotten night city editor Robert G. Hutton, and left him sleeping it off under a table.

Bob Hutton was a lovable drunk, a veteran of the old *World* which produced many distinguished newsmen. Every payday he would get smashed at Sonsire's. A fellow cub, Al Jaffe, and I would haul him out of the bar. (We heard later that the bartenders thought we were his children. We were, editorially speaking.)

After dragging him across Fulton Street to the White Castle for tomato juice and coffee, we'd lay him down on the out-of-town newspaper rack. He would snore there, atop bound copies of every daily in America, until at midnight Jimmy Murphy, the scholastic sports editor, a former sergeant in World War One, would yell, "Attention!" Hutton would leap up, salute, and hit the copy desk.

Wearing a green eyeshade, he would read copy all night, writing rhyming and other ingenious headlines, often handing back our purple prose with a long editorial shears while holding his nose. This practical lesson in journalism simply meant, "Rewrite this piece of junk."

Murphy was a newspaper legend for another reason. Early in his career, he lost part of an ear when a Black Hand gunman mistook him for a surviving veteran of the old White Hand Gang, the Brooklyn waterfront Irish mob which once ruled the docks fronting on the Upper Bay from the Gowanus Canal to the Brooklyn Bridge.

The other major gang was led by Ciro Terranova, the "Artichoke King." These hoodlums ran things from the Brooklyn Bridge to the Brooklyn Navy Yard and eventually controlled almost the entire Brooklyn waterfront.

The White Hand Gang lost power after their leaders, Richard "Peg Leg" Lonergan and his brother-in-law, "Wild Bill" Lovett, were murdered. But the Irish maintained their hold on the rich Manhattan docks, spearheaded by the Manhattan-based Pistol Local. As for Murphy, the shooter later apologized.

One winter day on Lower Broadway, long after I had left the *Eagle* for Manhattan, working at various times for the so-called Hearst flagship the *New York Journal-American* and, later still, the Associated Press, I picked up a paper and read, "R. G. Hutton Is Dead." Bob had died, as he lived, in the newspaper business, collapsing of a heart attack in the men's room of the *Eagle*.

I sat down in the gutter and cried.

LAST LOVELORN EDITOR

When I joined the *Eagle* there was still an "Advice to the Lovelorn" column written by Mrs. Laura Wolfe, the widow of Dr. John C. Wolfe. Her pen name was Helen Worth. (It was an age of pen names. Janet Cook was the byline of Margaret Pettigrew, food editor of the *Eagle* and later the *New York Journal-American*, who was responsible for my being hired by the *Journal* after the demise of the *Eagle* in 1955.)

Helen Worth was permitted to send her copy down to the composing room handwritten in purple ink. She often wore matching purple dresses, dyed her hair a brilliant red, and kept her tiny room at the Hotel Pierrepont supplied with bourbon and magnolias, stored in her sink.

Nathaniel West, in his *Miss Lonely Hearts*, gave a macabre picture of a lovelorn column. But this was not the sort of work Helen did.

What fantasies of romance she recorded! And behind the scenes, how many marriages she arranged, how many children of temporary alliances she saw adopted into solid families! As a doctor's widow, she had solid medical knowledge and in an emergency, delivered the baby of an unwed girl in her bathtub and arranged the adoption of the infant by a Brooklyn judge. The mother was introduced later to a loving man who married her.

With her dyed red hair, wearing bright purple, she couldn't be missed as she walked slowly from the paper to the Hotel Pierrepont, resting her girth at times on the stone wall around the Appellate Division courthouse.

"George," she would say to her desk mate, George Mills, financial editor, "I'm just a weak Southern woman." (She came from New Orleans.) "Would you mind opening the window?"

Smiling, shrugging, George, who was gay, always complied.

"She keeps looking for a replacement," George insisted of her widowed state, "operating on the theory that 'Nature abhors a vacuum.'" Despite this catty aside, George, like myself and a legion of others, adored Helen Worth.

MEMORIAL IN PRINT

Her last years were spent in a vine-covered house in then-rural Fort

Lauderdale, and I noticed that she had the local young men mowing her lawn and shaking up the drinks.

I insisted on visiting her while Pete and I were on a Palm Beach vacation. She was wearing a deep cut yellow cotton dress, revealing acres of bosom.

When I invited her to join us for dinner at the Banyan Tree, she groaned, "Do I have to wear a corset? I usually only wear stockings and a girdle to weddings and funerals!"

"Of course not!" I said, but Pete, a fashion plate, countered, "Let her wear stockings if she wants to."

I knew she didn't, just glared at him, and the subject was dropped.

When we arrived, the maitre d' led Pete and Helen in as a couple, noting that their daughter (me) was charming. Pete, who was almost twenty years older, fumed, but after we were seated and Helen exerted her considerable New Orleans wit and flattery, all went well.

Towards the end of her life her former desk mate, George Mills, also wound up in Florida, on the staff on the *Miami Herald*. A true gentleman, he cheered her last years by writing a moving series on her career, as the last of the old-fashioned lovelorn editors.

PLAYFUL SOCIETY EDITOR

Helen Brown, Society Editor of the *Eagle*, was an impressive-looking lady with a prominent bosom and lorgnette. She often wore what appeared to be the tail of some animal around her neck, displeasing me as an animal lover who would never wear fur.

However, as time went on, I got to know and like her. She kept a bottle in her desk marked "Specimen" to discourage theft. In fact, it contained Bushmill's Irish whiskey.

Though well connected socially and an intimate of top society personalities of New York and Brooklyn, Helen had a Rabelaisian streak which was at odds with her dignified mien.

"Here's to a long, hard winter," she said as toastmistress at the engagement party for reporter Mary Egan, a prim young Catholic girl engaged to marry business office colleague Fred Winter.

In a trained coloratura she would often sing, "When the frost is on the punkin', that's the time for dicky dunkin'."

Borough Hall barflies always did a double-take when Helen, in a severe brown crepe and flowerpot hat perhaps decorated with a bunch of violets, hove in, accompanied by a good-looking younger companion and drinking partner, Jack Scherer. The pair often made the rounds before she would make her train to Saybrook, Connecticut, where she lived.

Rolling up his pant leg, Scherer would attach his sock to his leg with a thumb tack. This stunt would usually result in a round of free drinks. Of course, he had a wooden leg.

Many boxes containing liquor and luxury foods such as caviar were sent to Helen at Christmas in gratitude for her coverage of various social events. One Christmas Eve a rascally reporter on the night side decided that all of us should share her bounty.

He opened a Helen Brown box from the then popular Stork Club and distributed drinks and turkey. We were soon dancing to tunes from a sports department radio. Helen never complained, probably because she had so many more gifts of the same kind that she didn't care. Or maybe she never even noticed. Her departure from the paper was reached in an agreement with adequate financial compensation to her, on the grounds that her Connecticut residence kept her from "mingling."

Everyone laughed at that. Helen Brown was probably the best mingler the *Eagle* ever had!

A FALL FROM GRACE

William Juengst somehow wound up as religious editor of the *Eagle*. The father of five, he lived in a humble walkup in the east fifties of Manhattan. The *Eagle* marveled at the Juengst lifestyle which included giving all the children Christian names ending in "y," such as Beverly, Hillary, Jeffrey, Tiffany, plus the middle name, Noel.

Unable to afford a wine cellar. Bill was apt to overdo it when a celebration included free booze. After a brawl honoring the return of copyreader Johnny Maguire from the Army, Juengst fell downstairs at the IRT's Borough Hall station, breaking his collarbone.

My role as police reporter caused managing editor Howard Swain to send for me. "Get the police slip on Juengst's accident!" he said. "And report back."

I duly retrieved the slip and was appalled to read, "William Juengst. Broken collarbone from fall at Borough Hall station of the IRT. *Alcoholism.* Taken to Cumberland Hospital." I pictured the five Juengst youngsters standing with begging bowls in front of their tenement.

Back at the office later that day, I entered Swain's private cubbyhole and awaited his questions.

"Well! What did the slip say?"

I had already made up my mind. Since he didn't ask to *see* the slip, I gave the gist of the record, leaving out that one word, "alcoholism."

"Is that *all* it said?" demanded my boss, his fishy blue eyes penetrating my brain.

"That's it!" I said, wondering if I could get my old law clerk job back.

That seemed to be it, until his wife, Beverly Juengst, planted an item in Dorothy Kilgallen's "Voice of Broadway" column. "Religious editor of the *Brooklyn Eagle* mugged in broad daylight at Borough Hall subway station."

"Do you want to get me fired?" I asked her.

"I lied to save Bill's job. Now, if they check the slip, I'm done and so is Bill."

A kind of general apathy had developed by then, though, and—fortunately—the matter went no further. I collected fifty dollars and brought the money and one perfect rose to Bill at Cumberland Hospital. He was the only white man in the room of six beds.

"Send the money to Bev," he instructed, "and thanks for it and the rose."

I was invited to a little celebration at their apartment later and when I arrived, found Bill shaving over a sink full of dishes. It discouraged my eating or drinking there, but did not diminish my affection for this funny, lovable crew.

AMOROUS BAIL BONDSMAN

Everyone involved with covering police news in Brooklyn knew Ronnie Carr, the bail bondsman. Though short and possessed of sky-blue eyes, as innocent as any altar boy's, Ronnie was a tireless ladies' man.

It took all the legal knowledge of two good friends, County Court Judge Nathan R. Sobel and former Magistrate Leo Healy to keep Ronnie from being totally victimized by ladies who recognized in Ronnie Carr their immediate solution to the problem of rent.

Despite all their efforts, he continued to woo, win and be shanghaied.

Once he woke up in an Atlantic City hotel. Beside him slept a female not far from collecting Social Security. On the bureau nearby were a blond wig (Ronnie loved blonds), the demoiselle's false teeth, a padded bra, a bustle, and various other beauty enhancements, or substitutes.

Waking up, she smiled at him and cooed, "My husband!"

Grabbing his trousers, Ronnie fled. He had married the woman and Leo Healy came at the run. The marriage was annulled on the grounds of the bridegroom's mental incapacity, mopery on the high seas, consanguinity, or some other convenient impediment.

BONDSMAN IN DRAG

Another time, lulled by soft music, quarts of booze and the promise that lies in ladies' eyes (and sometimes lies and lies and lies), Carr went home with a frail sister. Sometime during the night's passionate vagaries, he heard that dread sound, a key in the lock.

"My husband!" was all Carr needed. He reached for his pants and his wallet, but could find neither.

He found a slithery georgette number, the frock his light of love had first enticed him in, and desperately pulled it over his head and went out the window. There was a fire escape and he made it down three flights to the street. He seemed to be somewhere in Flatbush, Brooklyn.

Luckily (Ronnie was always lucky) a cruising cab appeared, its golden headlights as welcome as a Saint Bernard to a lost traveler in the Alps.

"What are you, a transvestite?" demanded the driver, your normal uncouth Brooklyn cabbie, before opening the passenger's door and letting him in.

"No! I'm Ronnie Carr, the bail bondsman. Don't I know you? Take me to Johnny Calhoun's Hole in the Wall Bar on Pierrepont Street, and you will be well compensated."

Shrugging, the driver said something salacious and took off.

Once at the long-gone Hole in the Wall, Ronnie got out of the cab, followed by the suspicious driver, and banged on the door, yelling, "Open up! For the love of God, let me in. It's Ronnie Carr."

Suddenly a window flew up and Calhoun with a rifle in his hand stuck his head out. "OK, you bastards, I'm gonna let you have it!" he screamed. Calhoun was paranoid about being held up.

"Johnny, don't shoot! It's me—Ronnie Carr!" screamed back his best customer when on a toot.

"What are you doing in that regalia?"

A FINANCIAL WINDFALL

"There's my nut for the month," he said in an aside to Evelyn Calhoun, often called "Gromyko" by Calhoun because of her habit of walking out on him.

Ronnie Carr's custom had probably paid off more mortgages than any amount of judicious saving by pub owners, so Calhoun raced downstairs, let his suffering friend in and paid off the cab driver. He then got Carr a pair of trousers and a shirt and tenderly tucked him in on a banquette in the back of the Hole in the Wall.

Another night as the hours sped by, Carr suddenly found himself short of funds. Even his well had run dry since he had been buying drinks for half of Brooklyn.

He bethought himself of the Smith Street office he shared with ex-Magistrate Leo Healy.

Telling bar friends about the episode later, Carr recalled, "We represented the Christian front and money was coming in for these screwballs' defense. I suddenly thought that the mailman would be coming pretty early with a batch of cash, and went over to the office. But the first thing that greeted my eyes when I opened the door was the big backside of Judge Leo Healy who had beaten me over there."

A spellbinding speaker, much in demand at dinners, Leo Healy was also famous for marital squabbles. His wife, Gladys, fancied her portly, bald husband a Lothario and once climbed a fire escape in the Brooklyn Municipal Building on the off chance of catching him at dalliance at a District Attorney's office retirement party. Prudish District Attorney Miles F. McDonald, whose office was on the fourth floor, was not amused.

DIRECT HIT

One Thanksgiving the couple had a wild alcohol-fueled battle, and Leo, affronted, left. As he departed through the courtyard, he heard his name called.

"Happy Thanksgiving," called his darling as she let go with the turkey which was a direct hit, right on his large bald head.

Leo Healy, Ronnie Carr and Johnny Calhoun all became legends to the reporters who covered Bergen Street. They were also all excellent sources of news.

To the Shack came politicians anxious for publicity, cops who wanted a mention, and a variety of other people seeking a newspaper break for themselves or their causes. Because I was almost always the only female covering Police Headquarters, first Brooklyn and later Manhattan, I early on devised a protective cloak.

"HE'S OUT!"

Oftentimes the visitor could be sized up right away as a lunatic or drunk, without a valid news story. In that case when he asked "Is the *Brooklyn Eagle* reporter here?" or later, "Is the *New York Journal-American* reporter here?" or still further along my journalistic career, "Is the AP reporter here?" I would just shake my head slightly, and one of the men would reply perhaps, "No, he ain't in," or "He's out." Invariably, visitors expected only male reporters on the police beat.

Of course, if the caller seemed as though he or she really was serious, sane and possibly possessed of some useful information, I acknowledged that I was the reporter.

Male chauvinism rarely affected me. I did my work, was really devoted to beating the opposition, and was rewarded according to my work, not my sex.

But, of course, I was a woman still. It was probably inevitable that I should fall in love with a reporter or a cop.

I did—with a couple of each. Oh, I had had beaux, boyfriends, lovers, even a preliminary skirmish at marriage. I was so naive I wrote a letter to my first husband, Jerome F. Fried, relating that what had transpired was not what I read in a book titled *Married Love* by Dr. Marie C. Stopes. As we were both totally inexperienced, I don't know what I thought would happen. Jerry went on to join the State Department and had a distinguished career, and I often regretted my stupidity.

A CITY ROOM ROMANCE

Though divorced from Jerry and determined to stay single forever and become America's greatest journalist, novel writer and literary dynamo, I, like all mankind, heard the siren's song. Even usually stuffy Wordsworth stopped writing about fields of daffodils long enough to admit, "Strange fits of passion I have known."

And someone, maybe me, wrote, "Show me that man (woman?) who is not passion's slave, and I'll show you a son of a bitch." I was not immune and fell in love at first sight, and made a total fool of myself over a gifted writer, addicted not only to alcohol, but to seconal.

He was the immensely talented one-time foreign correspondent Robert S. Bird, a star of the *New York Herald-Tribune*. The *Herald-Tribune* was Mecca to New York reporters and I may have somehow mixed up my admiration for the paper with my passion for the writer.

Bob Bird was a dry, witty and cold man, a Cancer, and I have always shied away from that highly artistic sign ever since my unfortunate affair with him came to an end.

Since my eyes still fill with tears when I think of Bob, I guess it was the real thing, or as close as I ever came. Was it because he was basically unavailable? Or because he was a brilliant writer? I still remember his stories of the first atomic bomb tests in the New Mexican desert, reports from the troop trains, his tales of Romania, the army with rouged cheeks, and Queen Marie, with whom he had a fling.

A newspaper legend, whose name still appears sometimes in *Editor and Publisher* as a master of the craft, he was also an intriguing lover, combining his dry and chilly wit with romance in a way totally novel to me.

"I don't know if I remember how to do this!" might be his prelude to lovemaking.

Until our encounter, he always had ladies with unusual first names. His first wife was Aloha, his second, Hester, and a long-time girlfriend's name was India McIntosh. I may have been the only one with an average name. I was also the only one who did not keep trying to renew our love affair, requiring him to get a restraining order after it ended.

My most passionate romance began on an appropriately torrid summer day in Brooklyn when I was assigned to interview the widow of Jacob Riis, famed muckraker and author of *Up from Mulberry Street.*

As I approached Saint Peter Claver's, a major African-American church in Bedford-Stuyvesant, I saw Monsignor James Asip in a black cassock playing ball with some African-American kids. He dropped the ball and a lean, brown-haired man in a tan covert cloth suit sprang gracefully forward and retrieved it, returning it with a charming smile to a youngster. That was Bird. I was twenty-one or twenty-two. He was at least fifteen years older. And I was *locamente enamorado.*

Mrs. Riis was playing the piano at the community center of the church and we waited for her to finish playing before the interview. Children gathered around her, singing, "Oh, What a Beautiful Morning" from *Oklahoma.* I have always identified the tune with Bird and a wild romance. I had thought I was immune to passion and love at first sight. I was wrong.

It wasn't long before I was in bed with him at the Hotel Winslow where he lived. We both drank too much for sustained romance. He finally joined AA and met and married a Brooklyn Heights socialite.

Twenty years later, as public relations director of the Girls' Clubs of America, I was hostess one dreamy, sultry summer day in New York at a press party at our headquarters on East Sixty-Third Street on Manhattan's fashionable East Side. My name was on the invitation list which covered all New York press.

Bird, at this time a senior editor of the *Saturday Evening Post,* apparently was on the mailing list.

My heart nearly stopped when I saw his elegant form languidly occupying a chintzy stuffed chair in our parlor. "How's Hester?" I asked.

Those grey-blue measuring eyes met mine.

"Actually, we're divorced," he said in his dry way. He gave me his phone number. He had fallen off the wagon and Hester had obtained a divorce.

He related that he was on the dais at a reception at the Brooklyn Museum, honoring him as well as others who had served on the board of the Brooklyn Bureau of Social Services. A waiter innocently filled his wine glass, which he had neglected to turn over. He drank the contents and, the next thing he remembered, Hester, her brothers and a lawyer were at his bedside and he was served with legal papers announcing his wife's intention to divorce him.

I looked out the window of the parlor where we were speaking. There was a light breeze shaking the emerald green leaves of the plane tree outside the window. A yellow cab went by. New York was basking in a gorgeous day of full summer. I felt transported, slightly dazed. I knew I was about to do something silly, something I would regret.

But I took the phone number he handed me and put it in my wallet

A few nights later at the Overseas Press Club, then at 54 West Fortieth Street, I kept reading the number over and over. Finally, my infatuation conquered my small supply of common sense and took over. I called and he answered the phone.

"Why not come over?" asked the dry voice.

New York was in flower that night. The trees were in full leaf. There were pocket garden plots of petunias, impatiens, daisies and marigolds in front of many buildings. The city dazzled with light reflected in the puddles remaining from an afternoon sun shower. I felt splinters in my heart, could hardly breathe.

Instead of taking a cab, a bus or the subway, I ran the six blocks downtown and a few more crosstown, from 54 West Fortieth Street to the high brick building at the corner of Thirty-Fourth Street and Lexington Avenue where he was living, next door to his dying brother. I reminded myself of a character in a great short story, Irwin Shaw's "Search Through the Streets of the City" or Whitman's "Mad Naked Summer Night." For once I was part of that summer night, not an onlooker, holding a mirror up to life.

Though I knew I had lost my much valued control, I could do nothing about it.

I was in bed with him in five minutes and we were back where we had left off twenty years ago.

I worked with Bird on stories he was then turning out for the *Saturday Evening Post* as senior editor. I filled his apartment with flowers: nicotiana, roses, carnations, spicy and fragrant tokens of my joy at our reunion. I was crazy in love and all the racing around was easy with him at the end of the rainbow.

On the morning of June 6th, 1968, I woke him to tell him that Robert Kennedy had been shot.

"An Arab did it," he sleepily responded. He had covered the Eichmann trial in Israel. The arrest and conviction of Sirhan Bishara Sirhan proved him right.

But he was taking red pills I later found to be seconal by the handful, plus alcohol, and we finally had a bitter fight and broke up. He sneered at Phyllis Twachtman and her gay pal, Richard Gaffney, who tracked us to a bar one night and were foolishly playful with the austere writer, and I correctly branded him a snob.

Then he thought someone had taken his wallet, which he found later after his sister-in-law insisted that he search other suit pockets. I left.

"Where are you going?" he asked.

"Out to the nearest bar."

"That's where you belong anyway!" he said, and I was through.

He came over to the Hotel Iroquois to return some books a few weeks later, and I was aloof. I had managed to diet off ten pounds, was wearing a white suit with my hair done, and looked my best.

After leaving, he returned at once, saying he was afraid he would find a woman in a green bathtub if he opened the hall door leading to the elevator. I had my son, Peter, then thirteen, show him the way to the elevator. I never saw or contacted him again.

I tried to console myself afterwards, trying to convince myself that he had become a cranky old man demanding coddled eggs and specially prepared calf's liver. But nothing helped. I still burned.

SUMMER DAYS

A friend, Joe Faulkner, called me when Bird died of a cerebral hemorrhage in a Third Avenue fish restaurant we used to frequent on the corner near his apartment house. How did Joe know of our love affair, I wondered. Then I remembered that my heartbreak was reported by none other than myself in a thinly disguised love story called "A City Room Romance" which I used to patch a hole in a weekly, "The New York Column," I edited before quitting New York for the *Orlando Sentinel*.

I went to the funeral parlor, met his sister, and left off a spray of yellow roses with the message, "Remembering Summer days a long time ago." I still think of him with bittersweet pangs, and wish things had worked out. If everyone has had one hopeless love, giving as much pain as joy, he was certainly mine.

BOB BIRD CASE

The Bob Bird Case made newspaper history. Bird was drunk in Bleeck's or the Artists and Writers Club just under the *Herald-Tribune* when a copy boy approached and told him he was assigned to cover the return of General Douglas MacArthur. He tucked the assignment order from city editor Joseph Hershberg in Bird's pocket.

The next morning, Bird appeared as usual at eleven o'clock in the City Room.

"What are you doing here? You're supposed to be covering MacArthur!"

Though Hershberg fired him, the Newspaper Guild won the case for the writer on the grounds that he was entitled to be drunk on his own time.

In between my two-decades-apart romances with Bird, the handsome Peter E. Terranova, then a Lieutenant of Detectives, and I became lovers. He was having marital trouble, we found each other's company exciting, and not surprisingly found out later that we had very little in common.

As commander of the Seventy-First or Empire Boulevard detectives, Pete was very popular. He let all the cops into the ball games free since Ebbets Field was in his precinct.

BEST DRESSED COP

While covering homicides in the Seventy-First or Empire Boulevard precinct, I seemed frequently to run into a tall, good-looking, impeccably dressed detective boss.

He had a crony named Sabbatino and I got them mixed up. "Inspector Sabbatino," I was apt to say, "have you seen my photographer?"

"Your cameraman is in that hallway, photographing the dead woman, and my name is Pete Terranova," he would correct me. He was then a lieutenant in charge of the detective squad at the Seventy-First. There were a number of corpses we met over before we began dating. Pete's most famous arrest was that of Waxey Gordon. A bribe of $25,000 to forget this "collar" was turned down.

Pete was a good boss—tolerant, yet demanding. He often spoke of one detective who was a lovable headache. "'Sleepy' McGowan shackled some bum to the radiator, went home and lost the key. A big case broke, the DA came to my office to interview the suspect and there's this petty thief chained to the radiator. The locksmith sawed him loose but it made a hell of a racket."

Pete checked out stakeouts faithfully as part of his job as commander of the squad.

"McGowan was assigned to hide behind a screen in a liquor store that had been held up a couple of times," he told me. "When I entered the store tonight I heard snoring. McGowan was dead to the world. I felt like firing a gun to wake him up."

He and his men handled and solved the felony murder of the sixteen-year-old Selma Graff who lived at 143 East Ninety-Sixth Street in East Flatbush.

LILAC TWIG CLUE

A lilac twig, used by the murderer to hold back a window shade as he entered the house to rob the occupants, was the clue that led Pete to arrest eighteen-year-old Samuel Tito Williams of 122 Sutter Avenue in East New York which, despite its name, was in Brooklyn. I wrote the case up and we started dating. One night, as we were necking in his grey roadster near the ocean, a uniformed cop came up and started giving Pete a talking-to. Since my beau was in the detective bureau, he was not in uniform. But he unwrapped his lanky frame and went out to talk to the officer. I caught a gleam in the moonlight as he showed the man his gold badge. The policeman went off on his motorcycle.

The paper was bemused by this romance. Pete would drive up on the sidewalk to call for me and I noticed that the police were very respectful.

The wedding of a reporter and detective boss in September, 1951 received a lot of editorial attention, including Walter Winchell's column and Frank Sullivan's Christmas jingle in *The New Yorker*. I think the line was, "Appropriate angels hover over / Jeanne and Peter Terranova."

My two children, Peter and Sheila Terranova Beasley, are the products of that marriage. Peter and I unfortunately fell out of love, due most likely to my drinking which became pathological during our ten years of marriage. I obtained a divorce in Reno, he secured a separation in New York, but we were good friends still when he died September 3rd, 1968, of leukemia.

COVERING THE WATERFRONT

I still covered homicides from time to time, but my final assignment at the *Eagle* was ship news. This was a beat at which you met the famous in a frolicsome unbuttoned state, just getting up in the morning.

Boarding the six a.m. Coast Guard cutter from the foot of Wall Street, the ship news reporters rode out to the Narrows.

SCALING SHIP LADDERS

After going over a narrow catwalk, climbing up a ladder, or crossing a gangplank, we boarded the ships and with passengers and crew, sailed up the North River, sometimes heralded by geysers and cataracts of water from saluting fireboats.

Sir Winston Churchill arrived on the Cunard Line's *Queen Mary*. "Ladies and Gentlemen, how nice it is to see you once again!" was his greeting. As I was the only woman, the "Ladies" apparently applied to me.

Meeting the legendary prime minister, soldier and author who guided Britain through the Second World War (and as he wrote in the preface to *The Gathering Storm*, perhaps the only man to have passed through the two supreme cataclysms of recorded history in high cabinet office) impressed us all.

The first time he was accompanied at the press conference by Anthony Eden, the second time by Lady Churchill. The Yalta Conference strategist was lively and quick, though no earthshaking news was disclosed.

"How do you keep your energy at such a high level, Sir?" I asked.

"I lie down flat for about twenty minutes at midday," Churchill said. "I am totally relaxed. This renews my energy. And it can be done anywhere."

Lady Churchill smiled and whispered something. "Oh, yes," he said. "And my painting, of course."

Told by a Cunard Line press representative that I was with the *Brooklyn Daily Eagle*, Churchill asked if I knew that his mother was born in Brooklyn.

"Yes, Sir Winston, and I have visited her birthplace," I told the great British leader. His mother, Jennie Jerome, was born in 1854 at 197 Amity Street (once number 8) near Court, not far from the *Eagle*, though a plaque identified a house at various times number 246 or 292 Henry Street, as her birthplace. In Brooklyn, street numbers were often changed over the years. (The family had indeed resided there before the birth of Churchill's mother, living with an uncle. My mother lived at 272 Henry Street for a while so the details of the two separate residences were familiar to me.)

I had actually done a story about Jennie Jerome and was flattered and happy that I knew a little about Churchill's mother.

A Cunard Line steward later said that, even though the statesman was nearing eighty, he still consumed a bottle of brandy a day, plus large portions of roast beef.

I thought of Lincoln's comment when he was told of General Grant's whiskey consumption. "What brand does he drink?" the Great Emancipator was reported to have asked, "so I can order it for all my generals."

BRITISH SLIMMING METHOD

The French romantic lead Charles Boyer gave the handsome Cunard spokesman, Jim Murray, a bad moment one bright morning by acknowledging that he took one of the Cunard Line Queens, instead of a French Line vessel like the famed *Ile de France*, because he had gained weight and had to starve for a movie role.

"As tout le monde knows, British food is terrible," he announced. I used it in my "Harbor Lights" column.

Later, Jim's daughter, Anne Murray, was to continue the family tradition as a writer. She was also a very popular president of the Newswomen's Club of New York.

As ship news passed into editorial archives, with Walter Hamshar, former ship news editor of the (alas) defunct *New York Herald-Tribune*, and Frank Braynard, master mind of Operation Sail, I was approaching New York's Kennedy Airport to review an exhibition of marine art by Jack Gray. (The paintings were being sold through the Marianne Strong agency.)

"Jeanne," said Braynard as the three of us gloomily studied all the arriving and departing planes which had made ship news obsolete: "Remember this. *It's only a passing fad!*"

The late Edward R. Murrow said there is no such thing as an objective reporter; we are all influenced by our own life experience. This is an inescapable truism. The distinguished head of the New York Zoological Society and author of *This Plundered Planet*, Fairfield Osborn, was a special favorite since he was an environmentalist. I interviewed him in his stateroom as he shaved, approaching a North River pier.

Later, as an AP reporter, I managed to get then-Secretary of the Interior Stewart Udall to pledge a meeting between the governors of Nevada and California in the ongoing effort to preserve Lake Tahoe from further pollution from sewage. The ostensible reason for my coverage of the meeting he addressed was a long-forgotten cultural event which I managed to squeeze into the last paragraph of my own dispatch.

TRULY EXCLUSIVE

Frank Flynn of the *New York Mirror* once got a real exclusive—a tip on a murder which hadn't even been discovered at the time and turned out to be from a really good source, the murderer.

His informant was washing his hands in our sink when he advised Frank of a body in an East New York park. When Frank tried to check it out, it was news to the Seventy-Fifth Precinct.

A tall, gangling Irish-American with a lock of dark hair in his eyes, Frank was a naive innocent although probably then in his late forties. A mischievous colleague. Walter Crosby, used to tease Frank by claiming that his sacred idol, General Douglas MacArthur, was "a muff diver," or given to practicing cunnilingus. Flynn, the brother of a judge and a devout Catholic, would caper about outraged, almost speechless with rage and disgust, while we calloused souls laughed at both of them.

THE CASUALTY LISTS

Not all the assignments were fun and games. Grim lists of the missing, wounded and dead soldiers, sailors and marines came over the wire daily. Families received the news by telegram.

Newspapers got the names and addresses over the wire after the families had been notified.

Not always, though.

Like all the reporters, I was assigned names and addresses. I'd climb tenement stairs to hear the weeping of a heartbroken mother, the cries of anguish, the pathetic "if only"s. The family had been notified by wire.

A Queens address in plush Jamaica Estates proved the exception. The well-dressed lady of the house, slim, well coiffed and composed, was certainly unaware of her terrible loss.

After some chatter about her son, she suddenly asked, "Why are you here?"

"We're doing features about local boys in the service," I improvised.

But the boy's stepfather was suspicious. He followed me out to the street.

"Is anything wrong?" he asked.

"I hope not," I said, fighting back rare tears.

"Could you check with the War Department?"

"Sure, soon as I get back," I promised.

"I'll call from a garage, so she won't hear me," he told me.

When he phoned, I sadly told him that his stepson was indeed dead, and that a contrite War Department would be notifying the family. Goofs like these led to the later method of sending soldiers in uniform to notify families of their loss. But in the forties, Western Union delivered the terrible news.

"I'm from the *Brooklyn Eagle*," I'd murmur, wishing I was anywhere else on earth. The reaction might be anything from tears or hysteria to a desire to talk, to provide a picture and information for an obituary, showing love and respect for the lost young man.

But once, before I finished my meek announcement, a stout woman picked up a broom and took off after me, chasing me down a flight of tenement stairs. I luckily was both slim and fast and made the steps three at a time, landing out in the middle of East New York on Pitkin Avenue. Pushcarts lined the street in those far-gone days, but I wasn't interested in them or what they offered. A bar was my goal and I finally found one, turning in at an inviting dark, cool oasis. I asked the bartender to look and see if a big fat woman was following me with a broom. I knew he thought I had the DTs, but he humored me and looked.

"No," he told me with a dumbfounded "Now-I've-seen-everything!" gaze. I showed him my press card, explained what had happened, and downed several double icy Tom Collinses before taking the ancient (even in those days) El back to the *Eagle*.

"I don't care about the ten thousand dollars!" another bereaved parent kept repeating. (This was the amount the government paid on the loss of a soldier son.) He sat on a cracker box in front of his shabby tailor shop in Brownsville, home of Murder Incorporated, where a slimy gang killed for money.

My blood ran cold. I shivered, even though it was a sultry hot day with heat rising from the pavements. He did care. He couldn't help himself. It was the most money he had ever seen or even heard about.

Sometimes the news was good. On Wythe Avenue in Williamsburg I interviewed the proud mother of five heroic, bemedaled and surviving sons.

The *Eagle* had run a great picture of all five with their chests ablaze with decorations. A grandson wheeled around us in circles in the shabby railroad flat, and I learned only later why he and the bike were indoors and not out on the street. He had the measles and I caught them.

"ANYBODY FROM BROOKLYN?"

The war in Europe ended when Germany surrendered May 7th, 1945. Japan agreed to surrender August 14th, 1945, after atomic bombs landed on Hiroshima and Nagasaki.

The troop ships returned to the Port of New York and reporters, as well as parents, wives, and children the men had never seen, were there on the docks to meet them. It was a thrilling sight to see the great ships come up the North (Hudson) River with men in uniform crowding the decks—waving, laughing, crying with joy to be alive and back home in America. Usually Kate Smith was on the stringpiece to greet them, singing "God Bless America." Once they couldn't find her and substituted Margie Hart, a burlesque queen, doing a splendid, eye-popping striptease.

"Anyone here from Brooklyn?" always brought laughter, but also a few interviews. Brooklyn is, after all, New York's biggest borough.

At the formal surrender by Japan on September 2nd, 1945, I stood with rejoicing crowds in New York's Chinatown. Fireworks, the dragon dance and general uproar signaled the end of the war in the Pacific.

MOBSTERS

Like many news reporters anxious for a beat, I was friendly with racketeers as well as honest men.

I soon concluded at Bergen Street that it's pretty hard to tell who is honest and who isn't. Some men known to be gangsters I found to have more integrity than many bank officials. At least, in dealing with such men you know exactly where you are.

At Joe's, opposite the *Eagle*, I often breakfasted with a well-known waterfront boss, "Tough Tony" Anastasia, who numbered among his brothers Albert, shot to death in a New York hotel barbershop, and a priest in the Bronx. We were good friends and he gave me many exclusives.

I also knew ringleaders of the Pistol Local, the New York mobsters who controlled the big passenger liner docks such as the U.S. Lines, on the West Side: Harold Bowers, since dead of cancer, and his brother, Mickey Bowers, who died in a five-car collision on the Long Island Expressway. Both men surprisingly survived the usual gangland fate.

One day during ILA negotiations at the Governor Clinton Hotel, Harold invited me to lunch with a representative of one of the big Jersey locals. I accepted. I would not take money or free clothes or other offerings, but I occasionally would accept a meal. Other times, I would insist on buying drink for drink with burly men from the docks, which amused them considerably.

At the dining room table Harold asked, "Would you like a drink, Jeanne?" By then, my alcoholism was beginning to give me strong hints that my drinking was by no means normal. Meg Ryan's portrayal of a female lush in *When a Man Loves a Woman* was an honest portrayal of my condition.

So that day at the Governor Clinton I hesitated, wondering whether I would get the shakes, an affliction that often hit me. Finally I said, "Yes, thanks. A dry martini, twist of lemon, please."

The Jersey local guy ordered something, too. When the waiter offered me my martini from a tray, my fears proved valid. My hand shook as though with a palsy. But then, so did the Jersey waterfront figure's hand. Bowers laughed and ordered another round. The shakes were recognized right away on the docks.

Learning that I was going to Fort Lauderdale on a vacation with my husband, then Captain Pete Terranova, Harold asked me to stop by a dress shop owned by a friend, probably a mistress, saying casually enough, "I'd like you to have a whole new wardrobe from me."

"Thanks anyhow, Harold. Can't do it," I told him and then changed the subject. He never made any other offers.

NAME CHANGE ORDERED

When a man named Donald Nash was locked up—years later—for four killings, including the murder of three CBS workers who came to the aid of a woman witness, I learned that even gangsters have family pride. Nash was actually a Bowers, but he was considered too stupid to merit the name and was forced to change it to Nash.

In 1952, my windup year with the *Eagle*, I got a dream assignment: the maiden voyage of the superliner S.S. *United States*, star of the declining American Merchant Marine.

The *United States* broke the world record by passing Bishop's Rock in three days and ten hours. This made headlines around the world.

PETS ON VOYAGE

Besides cabling this worldshaking event, I was preoccupied with minor stories to fill my regular column, "Harbor Lights." I suddenly thought of the kennel as an original angle.

How were these pampered dogs and cats traveling to Europe?

I sped up through the ship to the kennel on the top deck. Gourmet dinners were prepared by chefs for these rich beasts and I wanted to take a look.

As I bent to enter the door to the kennel I met a smiling, distinguished-looking couple coming out. They introduced themselves as Ed and Pegeen Fitzgerald, then of NBC, later of WOR Radio. They were to become close friends and future employers. That meeting in mid-ocean on the top deck of the superliner is why today I am directing operations of Pegeen Fitzgerald's Last Post Animal Sanctuary in Falls Village, Connecticut, probably the ideal post for a reporter with a passion for animals.

After introductions, and a visit with their traveling cats, Pussy Willow and

Half-Is-Alley, we met for tea in the lounge on shipboard and became instant friends.

HIGH C'S ON THE HIGH SEAS

Another distinguished traveler, Margaret Truman, laughingly declined to entertain us with a few songs. "No, I'll save the American public that headline, 'High C's on the High Seas,'" quipped the President's witty daughter.

Disembarking at Le Havre with Irving Lieberman, called "The Mouse," my Bergen Street colleague and the renowned hatchet man of the *New York Post*, we took the boat train to Paris. We registered at the Grand Hotel since the Scribe, where I had first thought of staying, was fully booked.

That first night I went to the cable office to file my "Harbor Lights" from Europe, an exciting moment.

"Where's your press card?" demanded the operator.

I ran back to the Grand, took the creaky old elevator to my floor and then emptied suitcases before I found the card. I sprinted back to the cable office just in time to get off my copy.

Irving was the only other reporter who elected to go to Paris. The rest went to London. Irving chose the French capital so that he could meet a nephew, Marvin, who was stationed in Heidelberg with the U.S. Army and obtained a leave to join us.

I chose Paris because my father had visited the city while serving in the Army in the First World War. He made me promise to visit the Louvre and especially to see *The Victory of Samothrace*, or *The Winged Victory*, the magnificent statue that stands at the top of a flight of stairs near the entrance to the great museum. I made it my first destination during the three days I spent in the French capital.

Irving, his nephew Marvin, and I toured the city together and saw a lot for the brief period we were there, including the Palais de Justice, the Surete, a bit of the Left Bank, and Notre Dame, besides all we could manage to visit at the Louvre and the birthplace of Anatole France.

When I said I wanted to go to the Folies Bergere, Irving demurred. But he changed his mind. He and Marvin escorted me there and had such a good time, I had to beg them to leave. We took a cab around the Arc de Triomphe and enjoyed the City of Light at its spectacular best. We also had been quite a surprise to the desk clerk, who tactfully offered us a double, then adjoining rooms. In my atrocious French I sternly told him we were traveling separately, wanted separate rooms and bills. Despite all this, I found the rooms were adjoining. But we kept them locked—our relationship was purely business.

Returning on the boat train from Paris to Le Havre we heard a familiar voice intoning, "All off, Albany, Schenectady, Utica! Next stop, New York!" It turned out to be "Uncle Miltie," as he was known on television, Milton Berle, then at the height of his fame. With him was Ruth Cosgrove, a quiet, pleasant brunette whom he later married.

We celebrated his birthday on the return voyage and he turned out to be a sweet guy. He helped the careers of many performers in show business. For instance, Berle and his mother, by buying all her costumes, made possible the comeback of Lillian Ross after her recovery from alcoholism.

RADIO DAYS

My phone rang soon after my return to the *Eagle*. A voice known to almost every radio listener in New York, Pegeen Fitzgerald's, was on the line. She invited me to dinner at their "half-a-townhouse" on New York's fashionable Upper East Side. Of course, I accepted.

This lovable couple, radio personalities, long married but childless, had adopted the whole world, especially animals. They broadcast from home, at that time a narrow brownstone on East Seventy-Eighty Street, Manhattan. There they had assembled what I later learned was a typical cast of characters: homeless animals, a superannuated Shakespearean actor, and a pensioner who doubled weekends as caretaker of their weekend home on Hay Island. His buxom granddaughter served tea.

"What a pair of knockers!" observed Fitzgerald of this maiden.

"She's engaged," I told him rather stiffly.

"So long as she don't give any free samples," he said.

I was invited to join them, and I did.

The program was entirely extemporaneous.

We were on the air one morning when Fitzgerald addressed his partner and wife saying, "Madam, I demand an explanation. Every time I take that new dog for a walk, it pulls me down to Third Avenue, turns sharp left and drags me into an Irish bar where everyone seems to know it, and the bartender feeds it bologna. Can you explain this?" She couldn't. I could have, but chose to remain mute.

RADIO BREAKFAST TEAM

Today, nearly half a century later, I am still part of The Fitzgeralds of NBC, later of WOR, even though Ed died in March 1982 and Mrs. Fitzgerald followed him in January 1989, succumbing to cancer to the sorrow of all New York. The Fitzgeralds based their success on honesty, caustic wit and a love for all living things. They were never maudlin about it, though—always detached and sometimes distant in their benevolence so that recipients were not shamed or embarrassed. A card in their guest room read, "Can we be of any help? Or are you in enough trouble already?"

We stayed with the Fitzgeralds in a sense, whether on the payroll or off. Jim Gray, my former and final husband and still good friend, and I rescued Dorothy, a macque monkey, from further teeth implants or euthanasia at NYU's dental clinic, and have taken in thousands of needy beasts here at Last Post, including pot-bellied pigs, a sheep named Murdoch, and a lonesome goat named Cappy. But we are mainly a retirement home for cats whose owners have made provision for them in their wills.

In one week around New Year's, 1982, the year Pegeen opened Last Post, we went to the North Shore of Long Island and picked up Apricot, a twelve-year-old poodle whose master had committed suicide.

Next, a mother cat and her kitten, found at a construction site, were rescued and then boarded at Mrs. Fitzgerald's expense at Mercy Clinic, New York. Later that same week we collected ten dogs and three cats, all from one Marble Hill apartment. Their mistress was about to be evicted and the landlord really couldn't be blamed as the dotty owner kept them all in her apartment without any trips to the outdoors for natural functions. The entire building reeked.

The laughter of the Fitzgeralds still is part of my life as director of The Last Post Animal Sanctuary in the northwest corner of Connecticut. . . Falls Village in Litchfield County.

76

MISSING DEADLINES

Though I truly loved them and the work they did, rescuing thousands of animals yearly, yet the roar of the presses and the fast pace of a whirlwind business held me captive. At the 1952 annual Christmas party at Edith Barber's home on East Tenth Street in the Village, Marion Clyde McCarroll, Beatrice Fairfax in the Hearst organization, offered me a job with the Hearst syndicate, King Features. I jumped at it.

I remained a Baker Street irregular, still joining the first and last popular breakfast couple of New York in rescue efforts, appearing often as a guest on the program, forever their devoted admirer. I read somewhere that reporters live for the adrenaline rush that accompanies the furor, excitement, competition and pressure of big stories.

This must be why I had to return to deadlines, exclusives and the challenge of journalism.

TERRA INCOGNITA

There were countless other jobs after that, including that truly bizarre stint at King Features Syndicate where I was assistant editor of the Daily Magazine page and, worst of all, the food editor. With that totally undeserved title, I was courted by the fish, potato, flour, and other commodity press agents. I was the answer to prayer. Since I don't cook, I depended pretty much on PR handouts for my Monday column which went to 400 newspapers.

The only compliment ever extended to me on my cooking was that it cured the dogs of begging at table. Apparently, I didn't please all the readers either. One of them somehow found her way to the unmarked door and entering, asked, "Are you the food editor of King Features Syndicate?"

Removing my feet from the desk and hiding a can of beer behind the curtains (designed by Dorothy Draper), I reluctantly acknowledged that I was.

"You have ruined my life!" she snarled. "I stayed up until two in the morning preparing that French pastry recipe you had in last week and it was so terrible that my lover has left me. He said I had to be too stupid to live if I could turn out such a mess!"

"Maybe you should contact the author of *Tante Marie's French Cookery*. That's where I cribbed it from!" was all I said to her. She left with a few more adverse comments. This, plus an itchy neck rash, helped me decide to quit.

The phone was ringing as I returned from my farewell (Dutch) lunch on my last day at 235 East Forty-Fifth Street, New York, King Features Headquarters.

STRAIGHT NEWS

It was food editor Maggie Pettigrew of the *Journal-American* (Janet Cook in the Hearst empire) and former *Eagle* food editor. She told me of the perfect reprieve. The *Brooklyn Daily Eagle* had closed after a bitter 1955 strike, and the *New York Journal-American* (known as the Hearst flagship) was looking for a few writers whose names might aid Brooklyn circulation.

I was selected because of my near decade with the *Eagle* with many byline stories on a variety of subjects, including haunted houses, Jamaica Bay stilt communities, crime lords, treed cats, abused horses, shipboard interviews and amnesia victims.

I took a cab down the East River Drive that very March afternoon, wrote my first column for the *Journal* and never saw King Features again. The neck rash cleared up overnight. My galoshes and thesaurus may still be mouldering in a desk at 235 East Forty-Fifth Street. The same equipment is probably somewhere in the half-a-brownstone from which the Fitzgeralds used to broadcast, with Tony Amadeo at the controls, when I worked for them.

Long after days when I occasionally covered City Hall meetings and press conferences during the incumbency of Mayors Wagner and Koch, I looked into Room Nine, the press room at New York's City Hall, and found an old brown jacket of mine, covered with dust, in the closet. I left it there.

My picture and those of two other *Eagle* veterans, Dave Anderson, the baseball writer who was to win the Pulitzer for the *New York Times* later in his career, and political writer Harold H. Harris, were displayed in huge posters tacked up all over Brooklyn in the effort to win *Eagle* circulation.

For nearly seven deliriously happy years I remained aboard the Hearst flagship, as reporter and columnist for the afternoon giant, since gathered to newspaper Limbo.

When Dorothy Kilgallen bombed out with a snide column about Mme. Nina Khrushchev, comparing the erudite musicologist and grandmother to an upholstered slipcover with her ankles bulging over her shoes, there were seven hundred protests, including one from Cardinal Spellman. I was assigned as second stringer to cover Madame Khrushchev during her New York visit. I'm still sentimental about *The Music Man* since I covered the Russian leader's wife during her attendance at that play. The headline on my byline story in the *Journal-American* the next day was "Nina Charms New York in Four Languages." While I don't speak Russian, I have affection for Russian literature, especially Pushkin, and was enthusiastic about the assignment. During the Second World War, I attended interviews with returning servicemen at 90 Church Street in Manhattan, and they told of sharing sardines and vodka with the Russians at the Elbe. Russians and Americans seem to me to be much alike in their informality and exuberance.

In covering ship news, I witnessed the arrival in the Port of New York of a number of Russian diplomats and political figures, including Vishinsky, Andrei Gromyko and Nikita Khrushchev. Shortly after joining the *Eagle* staff I interviewed Alexander Kerensky, whose moderate socialist government was overthrown by the Bolsheviks under Lenin, on the stage of the Brooklyn Academy of Music.

While pregnant with my daughter, Sheila, I covered the espionage trial of Rudolf Ivanovich Abel, master Russian spy, in Brooklyn Federal Court for the *Journal-American*. It was a toss-up on whether he would go to the jury first, or I to the hospital. He was convicted, exchanged for the American, Powers, and went home to Moscow where he later died of natural causes. Abel had left his information in such bizarre drop-off places as a tree outside of the Tavern in the Green in Central Park. He made his headquarters in a building across the street from Brooklyn Federal Court, visible from the window where the trial was held.

He bowed every morning when I came in, and I smiled back. My gut feeling was that, as a Russian, he was a patriot, loyal to his country and therefore not contemptible like an American traitor spying on America—but, like American spies in Russia, a brave man.

NIGHT SIDE

A group of night side newsroom regulars pose with a message to one of their own, Johnny Maguire, serving overseas during the Second World War.

Standing, L to R, Robert Wacker; Danny Fox, photographer; and Jimmy Murphy, Scholastic Sports Editor.

Seated, L to R, unknown sports writer, Al Jaffe, Ronnie Halkenhauser (later Mrs. Robert Wacker), Robert G. Hutton, Night City Editor, and Political Editor Joe Schmalacker.

They're at the horseshoe Copy Desk in the fourth floor Eagle City room. 1943-44.

SHOWING DISCRETION

Though I was "one of the boys" at Bergen Street, I never intruded into the all-masculine beer parties reporters sometimes held at The White Horse or other local bars. Here a group of police reporters observe some long forgotten occasion.

Among them are, L to R. Seated, Bob Walsh, *New York Daily News;* Johnny Deraval, *New York World-Telegram & Sun;* unknown, and Al Davis, *New York Post.* Man, right foreground, unknown.

Standing, Brisbane's former secretary, Emil Steinhauser, *New York Journal-American;* unknown; Paul Bernius, *New York Daily News* photographer; two unknown reporters; Larry Nathanson, *Standard News Association*; and Harold Phelan, *Brooklyn Daily Eagle. 1943-1944.*

UNUSUAL ASSIGNMENT
Jinx Falkenburg, a radio personality and former athlete, is shown interviewing me as the only woman police reporter in New York. 1944.

BERGEN STREET SHACK
On duty covering Brooklyn police news.
Standing, left, Jesse Strait, photographer, *New York Mirror*.
Seated, back to camera, Charley Feeney, the greatest "pipe artist" in the business.
Facing him, Robert Wacker, and seated, Manny Perlmutter.
Note letters spelling *New York Sun*, a long gone daily, on window. 1945.

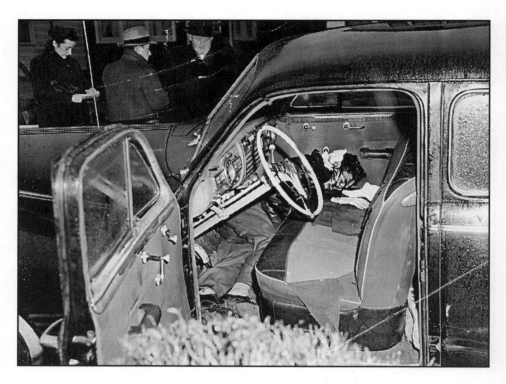

END OF THE LINE

Jeanne Toomey, John Feeney, *New York Daily Mirror*, and a detective at the dead end street in Brooklyn where the body of Carlo Zarcone, a criminal who served six years in Sing Sing on an extortion charge, was found shot in the head in gangland fashion. 1946.

MEXICAN ADVENTURE
At Las Fletchitas on the Pacific coast of Mexico. The noted
photographer, Mary Saint Albans, took this shot. 1948.

S.S. *UNITED STATES* MAIDEN VOYAGE

This photo was taken during the maiden voyage of America's superliner, the S.S. *UNITED STATES*. Standing, far left, Dick Harris, son of the chairman of the board of the United States Lines. Third on left, Ben Summit, *Life Magazine.* Irving Lieberman is wearing white jacket, center.

The four men, standing right, are all British journalists, including Don Iddam, the Walter Winchell of Great Britain, and Jack Frost.

Seated on the right, left to right, Marion Glick, Zenith; unknown man; Jeanne Toomey; Jim Duffy, *New York World-Telegram,* dean of American ship news reporters; Elizabeth Toomey (no relative, *UPI*); unknown British reporter; Cuthbert Maugham, dean of British ship news reporters; and unknown reporter.

Seated, left, Mrs. James Duffy; unknown; Norman Miller, *New York Mirror;* and George Horne, ship news editor, *The New York Times.* The year was 1952.

NATIONAL MARITIME DAY
Shown as New York Harbor observed a National Maritime Day memorial service honoring those who went down to the sea in ships are: Herb Schwartz, *CBS*; Dick Roth, formerly *Brooklyn Daily Eagle*, later press secretary to Governor Nelson Rockefeller; Jeanne Toomey, George Miller, *Associated Press*, and Santino Sozio, *NBC*. 1952.

WATERFRONT BOSS

"Tough Tony" arriving in Brooklyn Federal Court to testify on waterfront rackets.
"Tough Tony" Anastasia was Brooklyn boss of the powerful waterfront union, the
International Longshoremen's Association. His brother, Albert, achieved notoriety
as a mobster who was murdered in a barber chair at a New York hotel. L to R, Jeanne
Toomey, unidentified TV man, "Tough Tony" Anastasia and TV interviewer.

PROMOTING A KISS
Narcotics squad boss Peter Terranova is kissed by his wife, Jeanne, as she salutes
his promotion from inspector to deputy chief inspector at Police Headquarters.
                              —New York Daily News Photograph 1955.

LAKE OF THE SKY
The editor enjoying the incomparable beauty of Lake Tahoe at Al Tahoe, California, probably thanking heaven that she refused to handle money, only editorial work. 1964.

HEADING FOR GARDINER'S ISLAND

The cameraman on the right, standing, is Vic DeLucia of *The New York Times.*
Seated to his right is John McQuiston, Long Island Bureau, *The New York Times.*
The author is seated, center. On the bow, left, is her granddaughter Siobhan Beasley.
Others unidentified newsmen. —Photo by Jody Kolodzey 1989.

HISTORIAN OF LONG ISLAND'S COLORFUL PAST
Robert D.L. Gardiner addressing a group of local people at Sagtikos Manor, Bay
Shore, Long Island, on the 200th anniversary of the visit of George Washington to
his ancestor's home on April 21, 1790, as the guest of Squire Isaac Thompson and
his wife, Mary Gardiner of Gardiner's Island. Mr. Gardiner is the 16th Proprietor of
the island, granted to his direct ancestor, Lion Gardiner in 1639 by Charles I, later
beheaded by Cromwell. The author is off to the far left, listening intently and taking
notes.   —Photo by Chip Dayton 1990

PET SANCTUARY DIRECTOR
In recent years Jeanne Toomey has been director of The Last
Post Animal Sanctuary, Falls Village, Connecticut. Here she's
shown with Dusty, a favorite senior citizen cat.
                    —Photo by Mary Bond 1997

BREATHALIZER CHALLENGE

Ace photographers worked for Hearst: Bobby Keogh, Bill Finn, Robert Laird, Charley Carson, John Dolan, John Hopkins, the skinny elderly "Doc" Skinner (credited with inventing the use of a parachute over a camera for special effects), and the unforgettable Eddie McKevitt, a short pugnacious Irish-American with whom I was often teamed, were a few of the great cameramen I was lucky enough to know and work with.

When the circus came to town, Doc Skinner was a front-row fixture, camera at the ready. His ghoulish patience paid off. Finally, as he anticipated, a trapeze artist fell. The beautiful aerialist in her spangled tutu was caught by a clown in full makeup and costume.

That photo became one of the greatest circus pictures ever taken. It appeared not only in the 700,000 circulation *New York Journal-American*, but in papers throughout the world—from Tokyo to Zanzibar, from London to Moscow. All of Doc Skinner's perseverance had paid off—a dramatic, heart-wrenching subject, perfect lighting and composition, with a brilliant background of hushed faces against the garish circus background. The audience formed a chorus, caught in expressions that might have been composed by El Greco.

Assigned with McKevitt as my partner to do a story on the Alcohol Testing Lab of the Police Department, I went to Poplar Street in Brooklyn Heights. With the lab's commanding officer, Inspector Howard Finney, known as a Book of Rules man (in other words, always in an office, never a street cop). I waited uneasily for McKevitt to show up.

"Aren't you going to call the office to see where he is?" demanded an impatient Finney.

"I wouldn't call if he didn't show up for two weeks," I told him. "The law of the jungle."

Finney's spotless white shirt was starched, his brass epaulets shone, I observed. His uniform was brushed, his shoes polished. I recalled my husband Pete, who knew him as a fellow cop, calling him a fussy martinet and a pain in the ass.

"Where's that girl?" I finally heard a wild yell from the street. McKevitt had arrived. He took the elevator up and staggered off, saying, "I'm a martyr to science. I drank fifty Canadian Clubs at Sammy's Bowery Follies [that meant on the cuff—Sammy Fuchs loved the press] to show your damned machine don't work! I don't mind suffering in a good cause," McKevitt mumbled as he lurched down the hall to the testing unit. His wizened features convulsed in laughter. His face was brick red.

"By rights I should lock him up," said Finney.

"I owe it to Pete. I certainly won't let you ride with him. Pete would kill me. You'll have to take a cab or the subway back." McKevitt ignored him and called for the balloon. He chalked up such a high reading that he should have been dead.

"His pictures won't come out," Finney said smugly.

"Now there, you're wrong, they'll be perfect," I said. And I was proved right. The layout and my story ran a few days later. I mailed a set of pictures and the story back to Finney, the crepe hanger, with a note reading, "See! Your damn machine don't work!"

Finney called back to thank me, but added, "If a child ran before his car, he wouldn't have been able to stop. His reflexes were too slow." Finney was doubtless right, as Mothers Against Drunk Driving were to prove some half a century later, after overcoming a deep and widely-held belief that drunks were "funny" and anyone opposed to them was a "Bluenose" or wet blanket.

I seemed to land McKevitt as my sidekick often. Another time we did a feature on the Mounted Division of the Police Department.

McKevitt nailed the CO before we left. "I have a lovely rose garden back at me home in Rosedale," he told the hard-faced mounted man who was in full uniform, including hat."Where I could use some of your manure for fertilizer," he went on. He gave the cop, who looked over at me with a strange expression, his address.

I thought no more about it until I ran into McKevitt in the hall at the *Journal* a few weeks later. His pinched gnomelike face was red with anger.

"Where me house is covered from cellar to attic with horse shit," he sputtered. "Those fucking cops!"

"Well, McKevitt, you shouldn't always be looking for something for nothing," was my reply. But I patted him on the shoulder. Everyone loved McKevitt, even though the male personnel spent half their time looking for his car, since he could never remember where he left it.

Bill Finn was a lovable redheaded Irish-American with a drinking problem. Like all the *Journal-American* cameramen, he drove a *Journal* radio car. Once, having fallen off the wagon, he went up a curb, destroying a tire.

Photo boss Bobby Keogh insured Finn's future sobriety by a simple device. The photographers read their assignments each morning on reporting in, but paid even more attention to Keogh's scratch pad.

An inveterate doodler, Keogh always had on top of the pad: "FINN TIRE $80.00."

A marvelous photographer, Bill Finn died a hero cameraman's death—keeling over with a heart attack while photographing a waterfront fire from an East River pier.

A tall, saturnine Polish-American lensman was a tough fighter. I can see him now as we waited outside of a courtroom at the Brooklyn County Courthouse one sunny spring morning.

Mahar had instructed us to get a picture of a notorious, but so far lucky, felon who had finally been convicted but would be free on bail, pending an appeal. His yellow sheet was lengthy but he'd so far beaten the system.

"We've never had a picture of this mutt," said our leader, instructing us in the crowded huge City Room of the *Journal-American*. "We've never been able to land him. GO!"

We stationed ourselves in the corridor.

When the man we wanted emerged, as usual, holding his suit coat over his face, Frank Jankowski in one fluid motion slammed the camera to me, ran over, pulled the defendant's coat from his face, took back his camera, shot the picture, and we had again earned Mahar's love and trust.

"You two should be going to jail, not me. That's a violation of my civil rights," babbled our target. We shrugged, laughed and were off. The drive back to the *Journal-American* was blissful. We had once again triumphed, made Eddie Mahar happy.

Working with good-looking blond Johnny Hopkins was a pleasure. His picture of Kiendlville, a stilt community on an inlet of Jamaica Bay near Spring Creek and the Brooklyn-Queens border, remains in my memory as an artistic triumph. His lighting and angle turned out a memorable picture of aged wooden houses on a shimmering canal. Kiendlville ended up looking like a Dutch fishing village. The name was derived from the family name of an old East New York family. Theodore Kiendl was still practicing law in the area when Johnny took his memorable picture. (The small stilt community was destroyed when Starrett City was built.)

Johnny was later injured when, with Guy Richards, he crashed into another vehicle on the Merritt Parkway, chasing the Mad Bomber. But the Hearst settlement permitted him to open his own successful photo business, so in a way, getting very slightly crippled turned out to be a financial bonanza. As always, the Hearst Corporation was generous.

Cameramen are among my favorite people: bold, daring, really fearless, kind and often funny.

THE WORST YEAR

The year 1960-1961 was a critical one in my life. In retrospect it was one of tragedy upon tragedy. For the *Journal-American*, I covered major disasters like the double plane crash over Brooklyn, the Brooklyn Navy Yard fire, and a number of tragic tenement fires with heavy loss of life.

My first hospital admission for alcoholism ended my relationship with Peter, so my private life was foundering, too.

CONFIDENTIAL

Peter and I moved from our Bohemian stable apartment at 36 Veranda Place, Brooklyn, to an apartment in Stuyvesant Town in 1955. Looking back, I think this move to conformity was a mistake.

But we were there when a former policeman visited us and debunked a recent puff piece in the *Journal*'s arch rival, the *New York World-Telegram and Sun.*

This was a rave feature about plans for an exclusive club to be called the Ridge-Hill Club, slated to be opened in Bay Ridge with its own yacht to take members out for moonlight sails.

The visitor laughed and said that the backing was a group of Coney Island mob guys with criminal records.

Next day I did my research, checked out the ex-cop's tip and found out that his story was true. I wrote a hatchet piece on the proposed exclusive club with the yacht to be anchored in the Narrows.

My exposé caused authorities to veto both the liquor and the cabaret licenses for the project, effectively putting an end to it. Not much later, the building was destroyed by an arsonist.

The phone rang the night my exclusive ran. It was the informant. "Don't ever tell anyone where you got that story, Jeanne," he warned.

"Why?"

"I'm afraid my children will be kidnapped!"

I assured him that I would never betray a source, that I would go to jail first, as a fellow member of the Newswomen's Club had recently done. But when I hung up, I was scared.

Next morning I told our housekeeper, Esther McKay, to keep Peter, then two years old, and the baby, Sheila, just one, indoors for a while until things cooled down.

I heard nothing more about it until several months later when the phone rang in the Kings County Courthouse press room. Al Turk, a lovable drunk who worked for the *World-Telegram*, insisted I come to one of the judges' chambers where a party was underway. I demurred, he insisted, and I finally went. There was a table full of goodies and the caterer was introduced to me. He was called "Big Zack," a main man in the Ridge-Hill project. His business was located at the address on Stillwell Avenue from which Louis Capone, a Murder Incorporated defendant, had been buried.

Al introduced us, and Big Zack said to me, "That story was all wrong, you know!"

"You didn't sue us for libel," I returned and, glaring at Al, left.

"I could kill you," I told Al next day. "You set me up!"

Though I was wary for months, nothing happened, which I attributed to two factors: I was a reporter and my husband, Pete Terranova, was a Deputy Chief Inspector in the New York City Police Department, commanding the narcotics squad for the five boroughs of New York City.

UNITED-TWA PLANS COLLIDE

On December 16th, 1960, waiting for a murder trial to get underway at Brooklyn County Courthouse, I was sitting in the press room, gazing out the window at a dense fog, when the phone rang. It was my boss, City Editor Edward A. Mahar.

"There's been a double plane crash," he said. "A TWA and a United collided over Brooklyn. The TWA landed in Staten Island, but the United is right outside of Michel's in Flatbush. Get going!"

I was gone. The United DC-8 jet lay stretched out on one of Brooklyn's busiest streets, Flatbush Avenue. The sky was an ugly grey with a chill rain falling. Michel's garage was being used as a temporary morgue.

Everyone was dead except for one child. A touching picture of a passerby holding an umbrella over him appeared in the next day's *New York Daily News*. He told the good Samaritan not to worry about him, but the young boy was dead by the next day.

As I walked near the scene, taking notes, my eye caught a bright flare. Through the flames of smoke and fog could be seen a flashing electric sign, "Pillar of Fire—Pillar of Fire—Pillar of Fire." This identified a small chapel, a branch of the church movement or denomination called Pillar of Fire, with its mother church located in Zarephath, New Jersey on the Delaware and Raritan Canal. Mr. Lewis, the caretaker, was killed in the fire which consumed the church. That sign, which kept flashing as the building burned, was an eerie sight.

A Chinese laundry was also hit. It took weeks, but a *Journal-American* team finally located its oriental owner on the Lower East Side. We gave him part of a collection raised by my sob stories to compensate those who lost property or businesses due to the disaster.

All one hundred twenty-eight passengers aboard the planes and six people on the ground, a total of one hundred thirty-four people, died as a result of that collision in mid-air.

The only positive point in the story was that St. Augustine's High School escaped being a casualty.

My friend Virginia's husband, Johnny Deraval, a *New York World-Telegram* reporter at Bergen Street, watched in terror from his upstairs window at the Shack as the plane almost hit that high school where their eldest, John, was in class.

That period between Christmas Eve 1960 and after New Year's Day 1961 seemed to involve one disaster after another. Buildings kept burning. Mangled bodies and scorched flesh were my daily journalistic diet. One night, during this Christmastime, I was walking alone through the shabby refuse-strewn streets of

Williamsburg, Brooklyn, after viewing five small white caskets and one large one for the mother of the family, in a funeral home on Marcy Avenue, one of the long grey streets that snake through that depressed and depressing industrial region.

It was snowing lightly and the moon shimmered through the flakes. An el roared overhead and as I sloshed along in the dirty snow, I began wondering why people suffered such agony. A two-year-old had been playing with matches among their cheap Yule ornaments and the whole place went up like the tinder box it was. And the surviving parent was a drunken misfit, while the only surviving child, a sensitive young girl, had lost all her hair. The rest were dead, horribly burned to a cinder by the flames.

In that strange night of spangled stars and drifting snow, I saw another side of the coin to Bergen Street. Though cold sober, I was weepy, in a serious depression. What could be done to better the lives of this family? Why was life such a cruel muddle for them? Could anything be done to help the remaining child? Why did the hardworking mother die and the wastrel father survive? Did it mean anything or nothing?

LIGHT TO OBLIVION

As I trudged gloomily along in the already blackened slush, an amber light caught my eye. It shone over a neat white sign, "Ladies' Entrance." The old-style bars promised respectability to a lady lush with this sign. In other words, you were there to get drunk, not for a pickup. This stop precluded the first of many hospital admissions, this one to Brooklyn State Hospital, a devastating experience which ended my life with Terranova in Misery Manor, as I labeled our modest Belle Harbor, Queens, New York home. With my children and fellow lush, Charley Ward, I headed for the West, following Greeley's advice and the lure of easy divorce in Reno, Nevada.

When I violated all AA rules by walking into that beckoning bar with its orange light like a Chinese lantern, I was entering the worst period of pathological drinking of my life. The DTs became an almost daily event. But Mahar stood by me.

FIRST HOSPITAL ADMISSION

This first hospital stay for alcoholism was a searing experience. I didn't stop drinking, despite the shock and humiliation. It was off and on for years until 1976 when, hopefully, I stopped drinking one day at a time.

My husband, by then Deputy Chief Inspector Terranova (his final rank as the highest-ranking Italian-American in the NYC PD) placed me in this big city public institution for the mentally ill at the suggestion, he said, of a psychologist, Dr. Harry McNeill, but I always suspected he chose it to save money. Whatever his motivation, while it didn't cure me of drinking right off, it did cure me of him.

Despite my mortification and shame, one hilarious incident occurred at the hospital. I had done a story about the place in the past and Dr. Nathan Beckenstein, the director, proposed that I resume working for the *Journal* days, but return to the hospital at night. Then, he suggested, I could have a private room, eat with the nurses, and put out their paper. He needed an editor. He did have a cartoonist there (another drunk) and thought we could work together. I was tempted, but reminded him that I had two small children and believed that my place was with them. The psychiatrists there feared I could not stay sober living with Pete.

A GREAT EDITOR

Instead of becoming editor of the *Brooklyn State News*, I went back to the newspaper after this, my first hospitalization for alcoholism (though not my last), with the support of my really wonderful city editor. Edward A. Mahar had been a compulsive gambler and an alcoholic, but was salvaged through psychiatry. I owe my final recovery to AA and I owed my then-continued employment to Mahar, not only a great city editor but a caring human being. When I asked him once why he put up with me, he replied, "You produce, Baby. You produce!"

Coming back to the paper after the hospital stay was totally mortifying. Word had gotten around. As I walked up to Mahar to turn in a story, Walter Bazar, a really kind rewriteman, whispered, "Saint Paul was an alcoholic, Jeanne." I knew he meant well. Then, Mahar assigned a watchdog, Scott Morton, another rewriteman, to accompany me to lunch at the Knickerbocker with the dictum,

"Two drinks only."

He really was kind by being firm, and I knew he was saving my life, as well as the job, but I still felt humiliated, emotionally flayed, on exhibition as a "female lush."

As to that terrible fire, later, in Reno, putting in time for my divorce while working on the *Reno Evening Gazette*, I received a garbled letter asking my help in obtaining a wig for the surviving daughter whose hair was burned off in that tragic Williamsburg fire. It had been forwarded from the *Journal-American*. I called Eddie Cox, then Public Relations Director for the New York City Department of Welfare, and it was arranged.

QUITTING WASN'T EASY

More than twenty years have passed since my last drink. Years of psychiatry, medical care, hospitalizations and finally, Alcoholics Anonymous, worked a miracle.

Mahar, called the Iron Maiden by some critics, was my friend as well as boss. I liked him and he knew it. He told me once that he had stopped drinking and gambling when his wife, Edna, threatened to leave him if he didn't. He finally consulted a psychiatrist and found help. His hard-earned sobriety was also a relief to the staff, who previously would sometimes find an IOU for fifty dollars or more, signed by their boss, in a pay envelope. He would pay them back, but the loan was sometimes inconvenient! I had to go through more psychiatrists, a number of hospital admissions—six in one summer—and innumerable meetings of AA before I finally quit. Several times I drank, though on Antabuse, and suffered devastating reactions.

I still brood, but keep the cork in the bottle. I never have alcohol in the house.

Like all conservationists, I suffer to see forests slashed, subdivisions replacing woodland, more and more animals left without a home on the land they should be able to share with us. Alcohol used to dull that pain. Now, as director of the Last Post Animal Sanctuary in Falls Village, Connecticut, I do what little I can to make it a better world for animals. The staff and I put out apples for the deer and feed more than fifty wild turkeys through the long winters.

I have attended meetings of the Wildlife Conservation Society of the Bronx Zoo. An important cause is attempting to stop the poaching of tigers in India because of a medical myth that tiger bones cure rheumatism. And Last Post is a modest "Partner in Conservation" with World Wildlife, especially devoted to the effort to preserve the remaining wild gorillas in Rwanda.

HUMOR IN THE NEWS

Despite the tragedies police reporters deal with daily, there are many funny stories as well as the heartbreaking ones.

A kidnapping ended happily as one of our headline-grabbing psychologists foretold. A missing baby was found safe with a recently bereaved woman, the inamorata of a fish peddler. As predicted in a story I wrote based on the woman psychologist's analysis, the little one was in fine shape and had gained weight. The mother was joyously reunited with her child. A year later, in a sentimental mood, Mahar sent me to interview her again. He expected tears of joy and a saccharine piece about motherhood and reunion. But this was not to be. The joyous young matron of a year ago now confessed her desire to find a babysitter and go back to work.

This reaction was a disappointment to that flashy, funny ace newsman, my favorite city editor. He was hoping for a more sentimental story on the first anniversary of the mother's reunion with her babe. We managed to invest the story with some motherly feeling and left out the babysitting problem.

(We also ran my prediction on Page One, taking credit for the happy outcome when the child was found.)

TRAUMATIC TO SONNY?

Reading in *The New Yorker* about a child suffering trauma when his father's toupee came off in their swimming pool, I did a wacky story about customers who patronized a wig business in Williamsburg. Seymour Zee, a totally bald photographer, did two self portraits with and without a hairpiece. The layout got a good play.

Typos often seemed weirdly apt, like the society note in the *Eagle* which declared that "Mr. and Mrs. Brown announce the *betrayal* of their daughter." An apology appeared in the next edition. The *Eagle* also featured a head during the administration of Mayor William O'Dwyer that read, "Subway Toilet Cleanup Ordered After Mayoral Blast."

My favorite in a long-gone daily was a streamer headline which should have read: "Dewey Enters Manila Under Shower of Shot." An "I" replaced that last vowel.

The *Albuquerque Journal* rivaled the *Eagle* with such gems as "Woman Dies; May Live Here," and "Bedrooms Prove Quite Dangerous." The normally staid *Philadelphia Inquirer* ran such advice as "Travel Tip to Honeymooners: Go to Virgin Islands," and the *Hartford Courant* mangled an ad I placed a few years ago which should have read, "Are you the pet lover of our dreams?" Some careless printer left out that key word, "pet." Or maybe he did it deliberately, since it was February 14th. We had a lot of replies.

At a religious revival in the Bowery one night, a Salvation Army lassie was the main speaker. "Once I was in the arms of a sailor," she confessed, amid tears. "Then I was in the arms of a soldier. Now I'm in the arms of Jesus Christ."

"That's right, Lady," interrupted a seedy-looking drunk in the audience. "Fuck 'em all!" I couldn't use that quote in my feature about missions.

A dear journalist friend of mine, Joy Miller, was a casualty in the romance stakes. When Pete Arthur, New York Bureau Chief, became publisher of the *Peninsula-Herald* in Monterey, California, Joy quit her job as Women's Editor of the Associated Press just when she was about to get her twenty-five-year pin.

Since we were friends and she was immensely talented, I got her to write a column for me, as I was editing Jerry Finkelstein's "New York Column," published across Broadway from New York's City Hall.

One spring night when the plane trees were just beginning to leaf out in City Hall Park, we took the IRT Uptown subway.

Swaying back and forth, hanging onto a strap, I idly asked, "Did you ever identify psychologically with some famous painting?"

Joy nodded reflectively, and asked back, "Did you?"

I admitted that I had. She asked which one.

"*Philosopher in Meditation* by Rembrandt. It's in the Louvre," I said, adding, "And you?"

"*Repentant Magdalen*, also by Rembrandt. It's in the Wichita Museum," she said.

Joy, who always made me think of Botticelli's dreamy blonde rising in the seashell in his masterpiece *The Birth of Venus*, came from Wichita, a product of the Wichita bureau of AP.

BETWEEN THE BRIDGES

I still love the bar scene for local color and have some great memories of a few like the long-gone Market Street Tavern, known as Moochie's. This bar, beloved by Socks Lanza and Marvin the Torch, frequently mentioned in Jimmy Breslin's columns, was located on South Street between the Manhattan and Brooklyn bridges, a few doors from the *Journal-American.*

It was a regular stopping-off place during my six years and four months with the Hearst afternoon daily. Sometimes I drank with Breslin, then a sports writer, or Texan Joe Faulkner, a rewriteman on the same staff. But I was a loner and liked solitude best.

Ronnie Wacker, who was the prettiest girl on the *Eagle* staff, came by one sunny Friday afternoon to do some research for a magazine article. She wondered if there was a place where we could have a drink nearby, and I suggested Moochie's.

"The place is a sewer, but the only other gin mill around is Longchamps, all the way over near City Hall, and I have to finish my Sunday column," I warned my blonde friend, who always drew admiring glances from all males.

Though promoted to cityside, I still did a column called "Chitchat" for the Brooklyn-Queens section of the newspaper and my dear old paranoid former editor, John W. Newton.

Afraid of bridges and subways, Newton yet managed to function for more than half a century as a writer and editor, supporting a family of five children and his beloved Marie.

Ronnie shrugged and said OK so we went over, entering primly through the Ladies' Entrance, a tradition, guaranteeing privacy. Moochie himself served us, arriving at the table in a filthy butcher's apron, delicately carrying our drinks on a rusted tin tray.

"I would like to have more desirable lady customers, girls. Please come often," he said in his guttural growl.

"But Moochie, you haven't washed the windows since you opened the place," I protested. "And what about the sewer?"

EAST RIVER DRAIN

The East River kept flooding Moochie's basement, a serious problem since merchandise which would have interested the Safe and Loft squad was to be found there, offered for sale to in-the-know locals.

On the Lower East Side in that area of docks and tenements, their source of warm coats and hats was of little interest to most residents. Moochie shrugged, gave us one of his philosophical smiles and later, a free round.

Breslin's columns about Moochie and his girlfriends made Jimmy famous. One of my favorite columns concerned the time Jimmy received a prize—consisting of money—from Columbia University.

He related that Moochie, carefully attired in a slightly soiled tuxedo, accompanied him to the dais. When the official of the School of Journalism announced the award, Moochie stepped up to the podium with his best customer, announcing, "I'll take that, please." He then had Breslin sign it, and carefully counted out perhaps forty dollars in change from the award of a thousand or so, after first deducting Breslin's always heavy bar tab.

"Under her armpits, she's a virgin!" declared Moochie of a lonesome young woman I had described to him as very innocent, the perfect virginal bride.

The East River regularly swept in under Moochie's and the *Journal-American*. The newspaper pumped it back out, but Moochie chose to disregard it, leaving it to time and tide.

The East River Drive was elevated in front of the *Journal*. One day, walking back in the rain from Sweets, a Fulton Street fish house, the water backed up and poured over me, just as I was about to enter the front door at 220 South Street, the *Journal* entrance. Mahar looked me over as I reported in. "Did you fall in the river?" he asked.

Back home, my marriage was foundering on the rocks of my alcoholism. Since that incarceration in Brooklyn State, I had come to resent Pete.

RESIGNING FROM MATRIMONY

Both the Hearst Corporation and the New York Police Department had top medical plans. I thought he could have found a better wringing-out parlor than Brooklyn State where a violent lunatic had attempted to kill me simply because I was white.

Every time he criticized me, I dropped out. So far, I had dropped out of shopping for groceries and any attempt at cooking. The end of our romantic life came when after an ardent passage, Pete looked up and observed, "Those curtains want cleaning." I solemnly got out of bed and moved into the maid's room (with a Bible and a quart of Scotch). I remained there until my exodus to Reno with the children and Charley Ward.

It was July 1961 when I left the house in Belle Harbor, Queens, which I had come to think of as Misery Manor, and with my two children, Peter, then five, and Sheila, three-and-a-half, flew to Reno, Nevada, where I divorced Peter, who was retired from the police department as Deputy Chief Inspector and head of the narcotics squad. He had taken command of that squad just as the scourge of narcotics was starting to spread throughout the city and America. A capable administrator, Pete built up his command from twelve detectives to more than two hundred.

THROUGH THE MILKY WAY

The trip to the West was a success. I loved it. Flying through the galaxy with the blazing glitter of Las Vegas below, I looked at my children, wrapped in blankets beside me, and realized that freedom was more intoxicating than any wine. A favorite destination after we got settled in and I had a job was the "Liveliest Ghost Town in the West," as it was called, Virginia City. I have continued some contact with it and the Comstock Lode saga ever since. Thirty years later I am still dreaming about Virginia City.

Mark Twain's old paper, *The Territorial Enterprise*, was still being published. Bob Richards' *Virginia City Chronicle* had a larger audience, though, because of his lively wit and wicked columns. "Aunt Catty's Corner" was my favorite. A spoof of the solemn advice columns, it ran in question-and-answer form. (Richards wrote both.)

I remember a typical query:

Q. "My boyfriend wants to inscribe a verse from Pascal on my backside for my birthday but he can't remember it all. It starts out, 'The heart has its reasons.'"

A. "The rest of it goes, 'which reason knows nothing of.' And it's a grand idea for gifting," was Richards' counsel.

ONLY GAME IN TOWN

The only newspaper in Reno paying any kind of money was a Spiedel chain double operation. The evening paper was the *Reno Evening Gazette*; the morning sheet, the *Nevada State Journal*.

My own time clock suits me best for an afternoon paper operation, a vaguely eight-to-five or nine-to-six schedule. I am a morning person who for years has awakened friends at what I consider a respectable hour, say six o'clock, to chat on the phone.

So I applied at the *Reno Evening Gazette* and there met John Sanford, a leathery old Nevadan who said there were no openings. I had six hundred dollars and the name of a lawyer, Peter Echeverria, and that was all. I had to find a job and did, doing publicity for the Gold Cup Hydroplane races in Pyramid Lake. I had never seen a hydroplane or Pyramid Lake, but ground out a lot of copy anyway.

A GOOD FAMILY MAN

One sunny day, a sports writer, Bob Bohan, ran over to the small office in which I was grimly churning out copy and said, "Jeanne, someone's been fired at the *Reno Evening Gazette*. Maybe there's a job for you!"

After work, I got into a Whittlesea Taxi Company cab with the two kids. As we pulled up to the *Reno Evening Gazette* and *Nevada State Journal* building, I asked the driver, "Are you a good family man?"

When he said, "Yes, I have five," I scribbled down his name and license number, grabbed my scrapbook, told him, "Watch the kids, I'll be right back," and entered the building looking for Sanford.

Luckily for me, that year I had been awarded the New York Women's Press Club award for a series on the magistrates' courts, a PBA bond and plaque for the best story of interest to law enforcement, and various other Hearst commendations and prizes.

Sanford looked over my prize stories, cleared his throat and said, "I don't know. That man I fired was from Noo Yawk!"

"What part of New York?"

"Buffalo."

"Heck, that's not New York. I've never even been to Buffalo. I'm from the city," I told him. "What did you fire him for, Mr. Sanford?"

"Passing bum checks!"

"I don't even have a checking account!" I told him.

That apparently did it. While Sanford did not commit himself then, next morning the phone rang in the walk-up apartment where Charley, the kids and I were living, and the job was mine.

The people in Reno were wonderfully kind. They apparently believed that anyone who would leave home, relations, friends and a high paid job to gain marital freedom must have overwhelming reasons. And, of course, this was Reno. Divorce and the "gaming industry," as it was always called by Nevada papers, supported the state.

"Do you have a job yet?" the owner of a silver shop asked one day when I went in to buy a little bracelet for Sheila.

"Not yet."

He actually called the newspaper, mentioned that he was a faithful supporter and advertiser and put in a plea for me. I don't know whether that affected my being hired, but it surely didn't hurt.

SILVER STAR'S ANGEL

A good friend was Cherie Guild LaPorte, a comely, "stylish stout," flashy dresser with a big heart, a bewitching smile and a rowdy love of life. She ran the

Silver Star Nursing Home which took in older persons, an occasional harmless mental patient from the Nevada State Hospital for the Mentally Ill, an alcoholic bar owner who was a regular and an unwed mother, likewise a repeater.

While waiting for my final decree, I had the children in Fort Highland, a snatch-proof nursery and kindergarten with overnight facilities, financed by the gamblers It was a handsome place with a big fence, topped by ox skulls and supported by totem poles. There was a pet rabbit, a mynah bird and other creatures calculated to delight children, plus a registered nurse and a dietician to relieve parental fears.

I was told by the manager of the Holiday Casino and Hotel, our first address, that a one-time slot machine mechanic was assigned to run Fort Highland because he had a nice wife and four children. The gamblers persuaded him to take the job since they wanted a really top-notch nursery where the show girls could safely leave their children during performances. Gorgeous girls in full makeup and skimpy costumes regularly made a stop at Fort Highland before going on stage. Fort Highland was also snatch-proof.

Cherie had me doing publicity for her, while Charley was doing a bond issue. She let us crash in her office, complete with jacuzzi, since most of our money went to the children's bill at Fort Highland which included good food, and transporting Peter back and forth to Sierra Vista School. Sheila attended nursery school at the Fort. We visited the children nightly, saving towards getting a rental house where we could all live together.

CANINE TROUPE

Cherie, who turned out to be a great friend and a very funny woman, helped us out. She walked around followed by a troupe of yapping chihuahuas, cheered us with humor and a hearty welcome and seemed to typify the free spirit of Nevada.

The Silver Star was a wonderful combination nursing home, old age residence, rest home and haven. The food was substantial and good—hearty stews, hot cornbread and homemade pies. Like an army, a retirement home travels on its stomach. Louise, a patient with epilepsy with a huge scar on her arm (from suffering an attack while cooking), was the excellent chef.

FIREMEN LIVED NEXT DOOR

Occasionally Charley and I brought reinforcements from Reno—boysenberry pies, whipped cream pies and chocolate cakes. One night during dinner, Cherie suddenly addressed Dorothy, the lanky, blonde and vacant-eyed unwed mother.

"I thought last time was the absolutely final time you were going to visit us, Dorothy," she said, buttering a piece of cornbread. "That's what you said, anyways."

"Well, Miz LaPorte, there ain't nothing else to do when you live next door to the Fire Department in Tonopah," was her charge's answer.

The resident alcoholic occasionally decided to forego further treatment and take off for the bright lights and the nearest saloon. But Cherie had a sensitive electric eye installed. A few seconds after the thirsty guest left, a big sedan would pull up.

"Going somewhere?" she'd ask. "Hop in." And it was back to his room and sobriety.

A TALKING BLACK BIRD

We met Cherie because the dishwasher had a peg ragged-looking black bird, perhaps a starling, who talked. The *Gazette* sent me over to do a feature and Cherie adopted Charley and me.

Louise, the stout epileptic, and the assorted residents were right out of Dickens.

I learned there that Westerners were different. They or their immediate ancestors had braved the blizzards, the droughts, the dangers of the frontier, and had learned to share and cooperate. They were very good to me and my young children and I have always loved them, the late Mrs. LaPorte and her entire crew.

One day, while typing a report, I heard a scuffle and separated two men who were fighting in the next room over a pair of pants. Cherie warned me never to do that again, but to call a nurse since the pair were vaguely psychotic patients from the Nevada State Hospital.

Her latest husband (like me, I think she had had four) had a drinking problem, and often on the way to work at the paper in the morning I would see George LaPorte heading back to the Silver Star after a night on the town. He ran a construction company next to the rest home operated by his wife.

SMILING THROUGH

When George took off on a mad drinking spree, did Cherie cry inconsolably? No. This sensible, funny and indomitable woman took us all to the casinos in Tahoe for some fun. After George died of cancer following many final happy years of sobriety, Cherie in her last years found it hard to adjust. I am glad I managed to locate her—living in a trailer—and helped soften her final days a little with presents of candy and flowers.

"ROUGHING IT"

The spectacular scenery of the West had me spellbound. Virginia City, that magical town nestled among the High Sierra with its buried mineral wealth, continues its pull.

I still love it, often return, and still pore over literary masterpieces like *Roughing It* by Mark Twain, *Rocket of the Comstock* and other books covering everything from geology to bordellos on the Comstock.

Hoax and humor, a realistic view of human weaknesses, liquor sales twenty-four hours a day, as well as legal prostitution, all were new to me. And I was amused and captivated by turns.

In physical grandeur the Sierra, formed from a single stupendous uplifted block of granite, is the most spectacular range in the United States. Often, visiting a saloon in Virginia City with a Coca-Cola in hand—for I never took a drink there—I would study the mountains from a back window trying to see Mount Whitney, loftiest landmark in mid-continental North America.

IN THE CARDS

One day I stopped to see what a fortune teller in Virginia City had to say. She was actually in a tent or wigwam among the historic saloons and hotels of Virginia City, high in the mountains over Geiger Grade. She charged me little, and gave me a piece of advice—to get rid of Charley, and I knew she was right.

Meanwhile, I toured the cemeteries, copied the brief epitaphs like "John Kelly SHOT May 9, 1868," and made a modest living working for the newspapers and—on my second attempt to relocate in the West at Tahoe—Harvey's Casino, writing about the entertainers for Harvey Gross, the owner.

"I have heard it said," Cherie said one time, "that this whole road, South Virginia Street, which goes right into Reno, was an old Indian trail and that it went on into the Sierra so that fighting units traveled through there, tracking down hostile Indians."

Nowadays with the glitter of the casinos' lights illuminating the night sky, the Paiutes and their war parties seem very far away. Yet Nevada has many Paiutes, Shoshones and Washoes and their welfare is the concern of some humanitarians out there.

They have been cheated by the white man even from the breeding run for the cutthroat trout. By using water heavily from the Truckee River, the white man has ended the run between Tahoe and Pyramid Lake and Pyramid is slowly dying. I wrote many stories about the Indians and had an Indian, Margaret Street, living in the house, taking care of the children when they were not at Fort Highland. She was a lively, lovely, intelligent woman and a good friend.

TWENTY-FOUR-HOUR SERVICE

Charley by this time was running a flower shop, the Alamer Florist in the El Cortez Hotel. My father, the late Edward Aloysius Toomey, was sending his pension check monthly to help us buy it from Loudine Lovell, who frequently reminded us that she was "a true Nevadan."

Loudine, a skinny, hennaed redhead, came from Wells, Nevada, always referred to by her as "dear old Wells."

Like many natives, who did not have to leave their homes and jobs to establish residence, she had obtained five divorces right down the street at the Washoe County Courthouse where I obtained mine. Jimmy Lovell, her fifth husband, was dying of cancer, so she decided to part with the shop.

There was the flower store proper and a ribbon room adjoining. It was a good business and by offering twenty-four-hour-a-day service, we were making it better.

Since there is no waiting period for marriage in Nevada, we were sometimes awakened at two in the morning and had to rush down to the shop to make up wedding bouquets, boutonnieres and corsages.

"They're from Nevada, good as gold," was Loudine's usual comment on customers, job applicants, visitors, the works.

The implication, of course, was that people—like myself—from New York instead of Nevada were brassy tinhorns of some inferior metal.

Peter, recovering from a cold and resting on a couch in the ribbon room, awoke to find the hennaed old lady in a rusty black dress, going through her safe which was kept there. Piles of cash surrounded her and her eyes glittered, he reported later.

A miser, she saved money by washing her clothes in a freezing brook near her house, and eating lunch at the "Fifteen Cent Store," a Nevada version of the Five and Ten back home.

"Why don't you move in with me at the ranch and save money?" Loudine often asked me.

"Too used to central heating," was my reply.

One bright day with those clear blue skies overhead and a pair of golden eagles circling, Loudine came in to announce that she had finally secured a couple to live out on the ranch.

"And they're from Nevada—good as gold," she added significantly.

NOT "GOOD AS GOLD"

The implication was that New Yorkers were somewhat suspect, perhaps tarnished by riotous living.

114

A few weeks later she came into the flower shop, walking slowly, with a grim look on her leathery countenance. "That couple took off. They stole seventy-five dollars from my pocketbook," she confessed.

"I thought they were from Nevada, 'good as gold'?"

Jimmy Lovell was by now gravely ill. A thin, smiling, grey-haired man, always wearing a beret, he was suffering, but still at home. Loudine was feeding him dried codfish when we visited one day. That did it, and Charley took him to St. Mary's Hospital where he died within a couple of weeks.

I can still see him doffing his beret as he passed the flower shop.

Loudine had him cremated in his bathrobe and left the ashes on the funeral director's shelf because she was too cheap to pay the bill or have his remains interred or taken home. His sister kept calling up from South Carolina and offered to pay eighty dollars to ship the ashes, though she saw no reason why she should pay for the cremation. Loudine stuck to her guns and would not pay. Mr. Crosby the undertaker dropped by quite often to demand payment. Finally, one morning the old lady came in looking pale and told of having a nightmare in which Jimmy returned from death and rebuked her.

"He's mad because you won't ship him home," I observed. That did it; she paid the bill and soon Jimmy Lovell was heading back home to the southland.

NEVADA PHILOSOPHER

"He was a pretty good old scoundrel in his way," was the accolade John Sanford, editor of the *Gazette*, paid Ed Roberts, a former mayor of Reno, who had died decades past on December 11, 1933 but still epitomized the free spirit of Nevada.

Of prostitution, which was formerly permitted in downtown Reno in a stockade next to the police station, Sanford said, "You cannot legalize human nature. Prostitution is an age-old problem that must be faced. The segregated district in town with the police in charge and medical inspection is the one sane way to handle it."

Since the stockade was closed, Sanford contended, vice had increased, not decreased, with call girls everywhere. Without medical inspection, he claimed that disease was also on the increase.

Of course, legal prostitution continued elsewhere in Nevada as a matter of local option.

A complaint was made in Winnemucca, Nevada, about prostitution at a local inn. The complainant was a minister.

The Reverend's church job didn't pay enough so he also worked as a clerk in a local hardware store. A hearing was held and my lawyer, Peter Echeverria, represented the ladies of joy. Since the economy of the town was largely based on prostitution and the money it brought into Winnemucca, practically the whole town supported the women. Echeverria won his case and the *Territorial Enterprise* sold out an edition with the streamer headline, "Echeverria Wins Winnemucca Whore War."

(And the minister was fired from his hardware store post and left the area.)

THE MUSTANG RANCH

At last count, there were about thirty-four legal houses of prostitution in Nevada, the most famous being Joe Conforte's Mustang Ranch. When I visited, I found the ladies of the evening certainly were there by their own free will. Conforte loudly objected to a popular notion that the girls were enslaved, forced into "the life."

NOT "SLAVES"

"I have a waiting list," he insisted.

Don Dondero and I accepted his lunch invitation. An excellent kitchen plus ample time off were reasons, he said, that his brothel brought in the most attractive women. He also prohibited pimps from hanging around.

Those we met in midday favored spandex jumpsuits in vivid colors. They all wore evening clothes at night.

The cooks were handsome young men in traditional white with high chef hats. The food was superb.

When I complimented Conforte on his cuisine, the stocky dark-haired

Italian-American winked and said, "You gotta feed the cows good to get good milk!"

The parlor of this sporting house resembles the grand ballroom of the Jefferson Hotel in Richmond—opulent with paintings of full-breasted women in gilt frames, comfortable couches and chairs and lush rugs. There is a bar and men are welcome to just stop by and have a drink. Draft beer was three dollars a glass and hard liquor or a mixed drink, five dollars a glass. There is no pressure from the house to go with a girl to her room. Women rubberneckers are not welcome.

To my surprise, many of the clients were good-looking men in their thirties. "Why do they come here?" I asked Conforte. "They'd have no trouble getting a girlfriend on the outside."

"They don't want to bother with the preliminaries," was his answer.

Joe will tell you that a number of his girls have completed their educations at the nearby University of Nevada at Reno while working for him. He insists that one pretty lady became a doctor with her tuition earned at the Mustang Ranch. Since a "working girl" can earn in excess of $100,000 a year at the Mustang Ranch, his claim is plausible.

Storey County was the first to license and legalize prostitution in Nevada in 1967, though it has always been accepted in Nevada, a unique part of the United States which seems to be more like a small European or South American nation because of its liberal laws.

WESTERN PHILOSOPHY

On every subject John Sanford had an opinion, usually ribald, unconventional and startling to eastern ears. Of the country club, he asked, "Have you been there?"

"No, I really can't afford the dues."

"If you ever do go, be very careful," he warned. "Rattlers come down from the mountain to get the water from their sprinklers."

His list of rules was handed each newcomer to the paper. I did not keep a copy, but I remember two warnings: "The word gut shall not be used by this newspaper except as to cutting up fish. Fires do not 'gut' buildings. They consume them, level them, destroy them or just burn them down."

And, "All women referred to in this newspaper shall be regarded as ladies unless proven otherwise.

"Signed, John Sanford."

A lizard-like eye greeted my rhapsodizing over the extremely important federal job acquired by a local female resident, Director of the Mint.

Turned out the woman had been the very, very good friend of the late Pat McCarran, the colorful senator from Nevada.

To eastern naivetés, Sanford turned a kindly but amused eye. Gambling was "gaming" and the "divorce industry" was handled with respect.

A divorce turned out to be profitable for me. This was the Rockefeller divorce which left the Governor of New York free to marry his romantic interest, Happy.

MRS. ROCKEFELLER FILES

The phone rang in the flower shop one afternoon: "Jeanne, this is Eddie Mahar [my old city editor of the *New York Journal-American*]. Can you cover the divorce of the Governor? His wife, Mary, will be out there. Find out all you can and wire it to us every night in time for the first edition. You'll be covering for the *New York Mirror*, too."

Mary Rockefeller, a lady from Philadelphia's Main Line, was dignified, spare, quiet, disinterested in politics. The consensus was that her husband's political life was abhorrent to her and her shy and introverted personality was no help to his political ambitions. Her millionaire husband was also interested in the perhaps inevitable younger woman.

Mrs. Rockefeller's arrival was greeted with restraint by the local press. The divorce industry in Nevada was an important source of income for the desert state.

No intrusion was tolerated and the kind of rowdy press coverage commonplace back East was not encouraged here.

Her destination was a guest ranch in Verdi, Nevada, just outside of Reno: the Donner Trail Guest Ranch operated by the Dracherts.

I worked out a schedule between my job on the *Reno Evening Gazette* and my coverage of the Rockefeller divorce for the Hearst Corporation.

Days I spent preparing my column, "Sierra Sidelights and Reno Insights." Nights I covered news of the Donner Trail Guest Ranch and Mrs. Rockefeller's activities as she fulfilled the six-week residence requirement for a Nevada decree.

Part of the appeal of working in Nevada was the sheer physical beauty of the High Sierra. Driving nightly to Verdi, named by Italian railroad builders for a favorite composer, I passed snow-covered mountain ranges. There was a train of stars, near enough to touch, and their glitter, impersonal, remote, gorgeous, made a setting of unbelievable glamour.

NO JOURNALISTIC STEAM

The local librarian and post office mistress was also a correspondent for the *Reno Evening Gazette*. The assistant city editor, later top boss, Rollan Melton, known as Rolly to everyone, suggested I might get some help from her since she lived in Verdi and knew the Dracherts well. After a meeting in her small cabin, the heavyset redhead agreed to spy out the land for me and report nightly.

She agreed with a warm smile, but my heart sank. There was something missing. Greed? Drive? Ambition? She did not fit my mental picture of a lively, active reporter. She was anything but "keen as mustard," and being grossly overweight, might also be lazy.

The first night after our initial interview I rushed over from Reno full of anticipation. But, as my hoped-for colleague in tabloid-style journalism waddled across the floor of her small house to greet me, my fears intensified. A look of confusion, perhaps befuddlement, was on her broad, smiling face.

"Oh, lands sakes," she said.

"Didn't you get over there?" I asked.

"I mean, you said you could go to see the horse!" (This inept lady even had an equine boarder living at the very same ranch as Mrs. Rockefeller. He ate his hay next to her breakfast room. He might even have been the horse she was riding when the one and only picture of her there was snapped by Don Dondero, Fastest Shutter in the West.) "I don't know what happened to the time."

"Oh, my God," was my answer. "Please! Tomorrow get over there. You have the horse as an excuse. Then, just nose around. Maybe you could even go out riding with her and her sister. Find out what she likes to eat, what she drinks, when she gets up, when she gets to bed, what she wears—anything."

"I will," she pledged, with that disquieting seraphic smile lighting up her nice face, double chins and all. But she never came through.

Glumly, I went back to wining and dining the servants at the ranch. I was through with her. She lacked the fighting spirit of a true reporter. Maybe she was just too nice.

From the locals who worked at the ranch, I succeeded in extracting crumbs of information bit by bit. Mrs. Rockefeller rarely tipped, she enjoyed a few cocktails at dinner, she rode often with a lady companion, her sister, I think it was. I filed a report nightly via Western Union. At one stage, I delivered flowers (from me) for Mrs. Rockefeller, and later on got back a lovely polite note from her, thanking me both for the flowers and my forbearance during her stay in Nevada. For I never did get any copy from my stringer, hot or cold.

And my coverage continued to be respectful, somewhat restrained, and sympathetic. She was a nice woman.

IT'S AN ILL WIND

Mary Rockefeller's stay in Reno improved my always shaky financial status. I received some hefty checks from the Hearst Corporation. One tangible result was that I bought bicycles for my children, now four and six. Asked where they got them by other kids on the block, they answered, "Mrs. Rockefeller."

MYTHIC NOTION

All the neighbors from then on assumed we were close personal friends of the Rockefellers. I never found the time to clarify our true relationship-- hunter and hunted, or whatever a reporter and his potential news source are to one another.

Not only divorces made the headlines in Reno. There were feature stories that thrilled a tenderfoot: a beaver swimming down the Truckee River, Paiutes suing for cutthroat trout fishery rights, and a story about a descendant of George Washington, Dr. Eric Wilson.

Dr. Wilson, a retired gynecologist from Hollywood, and his wife, a former silent screen star, Pearle White (not the famous Pearl White, but another lesser-known though far more beautiful actress from the Oklahoma Territory) became good friends. They had a handsome residence on Virginia Lake, a high income section just beyond downtown Reno, but still within the boundaries of what is billed as The Biggest Little City in the World.

DUCKS A MAIN INTEREST

In his retirement, the doctor became interested in ducks. He had a bullhorn and to anyone he saw annoying or molesting a duck, he would call: "Now hear this! Dr. Wilson here! I see you and am reporting you to the Reno police!"

POLICE PROTECTION

I was often on hand as the call came in to the long-suffering police chief Elmer Briscoe, who would answer, "Yes, Dr. Wilson. I'll send a man right over!"

George Washington's kinsman was also a major taxpayer and great benefactor of all Nevada charities, including St. Mary's Hospital, the Nevada Humane Society and most important of all, the police benevolent association. When the Wilsons—rich as Midas already—won the Irish Sweepstakes, they divided the proceeds between the humane society and the police charities. Wilson was a sacred cow, a man to be reckoned with.

Finally, perhaps in desperation, the Reno Police Department made Virginia Lake a fixed post. The officer assigned was fed on lobster newburg and mountain trout and never asked for a different assignment, hearkening each day to the dinner bell rung specially for him by a uniformed maid, from the front steps of the residence on Virginia Lake where the ducks multiplied under police protection.

The Wilsons enjoyed us. We shared a kind of big city rapport and we accompanied them in their Rolls Royce to dinners and social events. At a benefit for the American Cancer Society, Pearle spoke of their maid, who seemed able to get drunk no matter what strategies were employed.

"I have the liquor cabinet locked up," she said, "but she went home drunk again yesterday."

"Probably brought a bottle with her," was my suggestion as I sampled some caviar.

"No, I checked her coat," said her puzzled boss.

"The doctor's Pinot water, or your cologne," I offered.

That surmise turned out to be prophetic. When she got home Pearle found empty a hefty bottle of Blue Grass and various eau de violet concoctions the doctor used as aftershave fresheners. The maid showed no ill effects, aside from intoxication.

Though the place in Reno was a lot slower than in New York, it had its share of disasters. One was the Golden Hotel fire. When I arrived there, fire engines filled the street and a plane was dumping some chemical from above into the heart of the blaze.

Rescue operations were still going on. A dark-haired security guard was carrying a heavy woman down a fire escape.

Other heroic rescues were accomplished, but six people died, including a beautiful showgirl, head of the Parisian Playmates company, exhausted by a night of partying and champagne. She was reportedly too tipsy to get out. She and five others died despite heroic firefighting efforts.

GAMBLING FEVER

In order to call in the story, I had to go through a casino. Was it Fitzgerald's Nevada Club? I think so and as I tried to pass the gamblers, cranking away at the slot machines, faces lit by the expectation of a jackpot, I marveled at their indifference to the conflagration raging a few feet away.

"Excuse me. Let me through, please. There's a big fire outside," I said as I pushed past the absorbed slot machine addicts.

I did a piece for *Editor and Publisher* on this addiction, after learning that some years before, when the Truckee River overflowed its banks flooding South Virginia Street, slot machine addicts had to be carried from their play to safety, resisting all the while, sure that the next crank of the slot machine would bring a jackpot, the next throw of the dice, a glittering harvest of gold.

THE USUAL HERO DOG

As the fire continued, I herded surviving showgirls, and the hero dog (there is almost always a hero dog who barks the first alarm) and some rescuers into the Greyhound Bus station to be photographed by a *Reno Evening Gazette* photographer and interviewed by myself. This was a Hearst technique, gaining an exclusive and keeping the story from the opposition. As I wrapped it up with good quotes, details, heroic rescues and gratitude expressed by those who were saved, I suddenly realized that actually in Reno, Nevada, there was no competition. The two papers, the *Nevada State Journal*, the morning paper, and the *Reno Evening Gazette*, the afternoon paper for which I worked, were both owned by Spiedel (later sold to Gannett). They were all there was in Reno. There was, in fact, no competition to beat!

And I had gone to enormous pains to beat a non-existent competition, just from force of habit. I consoled myself by thinking that the wire services and the *Sacramento Bee* were beaten. But Reno was not as competitive as New York, and I heard nothing of my coup.

"AVAILABLE" MAKES THE GRADE

The *Sacramento Bee* had a correspondent eccentric enough to rival any reporters I knew back East. His name was "Available" Bigler. He made headlines as the only person known to have fallen off Geiger Grade and survived.

I learned that "grade" out West described some terrifying precipitous roadway between a flat plain and a high peak. Apparently "Available" and his lady companion were so drunk they were totally relaxed. The car landed in a Ponderosa pine. Both survived. But when the story hit the newspapers, "Available's" wife divorced him.

The *Gazette* paid perhaps one-third of my old Hearst salary and I was hard pressed for money. Soon the paper learned that I was a hustler, hungry and always eager for any extra work.

"Toomey!" I heard that shout many times in many city rooms, and it always got me up and to the main hub of whatever newspaper I was working for, the city desk.

"Do you want to do a piece for 'Physicians' Legal Brief'?" They want an article on a nurses' convention at the Convention Center," Rolly Melton explained.

Or, "Something called 'The Veterinary Dispatch' wants a stringer here. Do you want it, Toomey?"

My answer was always the same. "Yes." And I wound up with some extra sources of money. The newspaper and its personnel were absolutely wonderful to me. The way of Nevadans, I found, was to make available, when possible, some kind of practical help. As a workaholic as well as an alcoholic, I grasped any lifeline thrown me.

ONCE WAS ENOUGH

Just once I went crazy on the slots. I had developed a personal affection for a double quarter machine at Jamie Kelly's Nugget, the cheapest casino on South Virginia Street, and often stopped there to throw in a few dollars. This particular time I kept losing, and I made several trips to the Reno Bank of Commerce, cleaning out our pathetically small savings accounts, all the rent, food and clothing money we had. I lost it all, but then Dame Fortune smiled, perhaps in pity, and I won every quarter back, plus a little extra, maybe seventy-five dollars or so. I left, shaken and grateful, with a number of small dolls. They paid off in premiums as well as cash. I went right back to the bank and restored our tiny savings account. With the winnings I bought the youngsters new clothes and some much-needed sheets at Montgomery Ward's and went home, chastened, really scared over this new compulsion I didn't know I had.

Margaret Street, who took care of the children when they were not at Fort Highland, asked, "What happened?"

"I blew all our money," I admitted, feeling pretty stupid.

"Not the rent?"

"Yes, everything . . . but I won it all back again. Never again."

I never have. Though I have gambled since, I set a limit and stick to it. One addiction was enough.

NOT IMPRESSED

Governor Nelson Rockefeller came to Reno on a speech-making engagement. His press agent, Dick Roth, with whom I had worked on the *Brooklyn Daily Eagle*, sent ahead a copy of the governor's prepared speech.

Following a *Journal-American* habit, I wrote the story ahead, from the speech, so that it could be set and ready to go as soon as I checked it out and made sure the Empire State's top executive showed.

Somewhere in the piece I had written that Rockefeller addressed "a capacity crowd." Once I reached the hall in downtown Reno where he was scheduled to speak, I began to worry. There was no one there. At last, Rockefeller, my friend Roth, and a few other attachés arrived and he went to the podium.

He followed text so I was OK on the speech, but there couldn't have been more than eight people in the audience. I put on my coat, got my gear together, and ran all the way to the *Gazette* on Second Street to change my story to "before a sparse audience," or some such, indicating the paucity of interest.

I asked Cherie Guild LaPorte, my good friend of the Silver Star Nursing Home, why so few people turned out to hear a famous politician of a renowned family.

NEVADANS

"Why, Honey, they've seen everything here. They wouldn't turn out unless you promised them an axe murder or a really big party with lots of free food and booze," she said. "The truth is they just don't give a damn!"

That was so. Nevadans were blasé. With legal gaming, easy divorce, legal prostitution and many tax-weary millionaires living close by, why should they get excited about some New York politician? They didn't.

My New York background was no help to me. Quite often I would cringe as some Westerner, after looking me over and listening for a while, would ask, "Ar yew from Noo York?"

My "Yes" became very low key. I knew that people from the metropolis were viewed with some suspicion, and sometimes outright dislike. Once I received a kind of compliment when Norman Cardozo, who later won the Pulitzer for the *Gazette*, came into the file room or library where I was painfully assembling the mandatory end-of-the-year review of the news and said, "I like you, Jeanne. Even though you're from Noo York."

I said "Thanks," and let it go.

Once I thought my being from New York was going to get me fired. Through some careless oversight, a letter from the New York Newspaper Guild was forwarded to me at the *Gazette*.

When I arrived that morning at eight o'clock, hours were long and the paper was not organized. I found city editor Rollan Melton (later publisher) looking over the return address on the letter.

"Were you in the union?" he asked.

"Yes. It was a closed shop, Rolly," I answered.

"You're not going to make any trouble here, are you?"

"Gosh, no. I just want to earn a living and support my children," I replied.

Nothing more was said, but I called up my New York lawyer later and asked him to show more discretion and either throw union correspondence away or forward it to the house.

An odd development followed, though. From then on I covered the Labor Temple for the paper, apparently because the bosses felt I might have some rapport with the construction, confectionery and hotel trades workers, the only categories then organized there. Nevada was a right-to-work state and unions were often regarded as communistic and from Noo York.

I never spoke of the union again, and heard no more about it.

Back in New York, I had once gotten a man off a chain gang. This exploit was possibly one of the reasons the *Reno Evening Gazette* hired me.

While covering courts in Brooklyn, I spotted a one-legged man handcuffed to a Coney Island detective I knew. "What's he in for?" I asked Detective Walter Duffy. (I was sure it couldn't be rape, murder or anything really violent because the man obviously lacked the physical capacity.)

"He's being extradited to the State of Georgia for theft of four tires and a tire iron," Detective Duffy of the Coney Island squad explained.

"I sold the truck stripped down," said the defendant who was named John Flanagan. He told me that he lost his leg in a sawmill accident in Georgia and that the owner of the sawmill was getting back at him for stealing his girl (even with the one leg). Now he was worried about his wife and their two little boys. He supported them, selling magazines door-to-door.

RANSOMED

I had a photograph taken and did a sob story on the case for the *New York Journal-American*. Money rolled in and eventually we managed to bail Flanagan out by paying the various fines, charges, and so forth. His touching and dramatic return at Kennedy Airport, greeted by the detective, his small sons and myself, was the subject of a television documentary by an old friend, Gabe Pressman, who had sensibly left print journalism for the glamorous world of TV.

I saw myself on NBC-TV in a program listed as an example of enterprise in journalism one night when I stopped off at a long-gone City Hall restaurant, Caruso's, for a drink at the bar.

The case proved that curiosity is still a reporter's best asset.

SOUTHERN PACIFIC SNOWSHEDS

Editor Bryn Armstrong assigned me to do a feature piece on the snowsheds of the Southern Pacific, suggested to him by a magazine article. I did my own checking, wrote a long piece, and it ran with my byline.

That year the *Reno Evening Gazette* won two prizes from the Nevada State Press Association, one for the obituary on Pat McCarran and one for the snowsheds feature. My picture appeared in the newspaper and in *Editor and Publisher*, bible of the Fourth Estate.

STATE HOSPITAL PROBE

In Nevada, the opportunity for some investigative reporting came when the paper received a letter from an orderly at the Nevada State Hospital for the Mentally Ill, located in Sparks, right outside of Reno.

Handwritten, misspelled, the letter told of atrocities allegedly committed against the elderly patients in the geriatric ward.

Enemas were given by hose to punish the incontinent, the letter reported. And old folks were put outside in the strong Nevada sun without hats so that one or more had died of sunstroke.

There were other charges. The probe was assigned to me, and I got to work.

A trip to the hospital followed and I started a detailed series on the Nevada State Hospital, covering the various wards.

In the violent women's ward a small girl ran loose, and there were various other charges of neglect and violence against female residents as well as geriatric patients. A hearing was ordered after the articles started reporting abuses. Attorney General Roger Foley conducted the hearing.

Doctor Sidney Tillim was the psychiatrist in charge. He was fighting for his professional life and he apparently did some investigating into my personal history.

"I was talking to Doctor Beckenstein about you," he said slyly one day, low-voiced, apparently thinking this would scare me off.

In 1960-1961 as my marriage was breaking up, I was, as I reported previously, admitted to Brooklyn State Hospital for alcoholism. I spent a few days there, passed up a change to put out the "school paper" and looked back at it with a kind of rueful amusement. Doctor Nathan Beckenstein was my friend and the medical director.

PAPER NOTIFIED

I realized that through learning of my hospital admission, Doctor Tillim thought he had a hold on me, a way of perhaps stopping the critical articles, or at least softening the impact.

"Oh, yes. I've told the paper about my alcoholism. They know all about it and also that I'm now in Alcoholics Anonymous," I told him. His expression of disappointment and astonishment is still vivid to me after more than thirty years.

The hearings found some culpability and resulted in Tillim's transfer to the prison, where he worked among the criminals there until his death. He was not a bad psychiatrist and ironically, was very good to the alcoholics.

My alcoholism was crouching like a sleeping beast. I did not drink for my thirteen months on the *Reno Evening Gazette* until the very end.

LURE OF THE MOUNTAINS

Story followed upon story. There were some enchanting visits to Snow Valley where the children got a ride in a dog sled, and to Mount Rose and Lake Tahoe.

I loved to see the golden eagles soaring overhead, and enjoyed arriving at the paper in the mornings to see the rosy petunias banking the building, the sprinklers going and that blue arc of the Nevada sky.

But one day Charley fell off the wagon. A cab driver arrived at the flower shop, demanding a hundred dollars. Charley had had him drive him around the Lake of the Sky and then read the Bible to him as he lay, sodden drunk, in bed. It was devastating and, alas, I, too, fell.

After consuming a bottle of vodka in the chilled flower case, I spent a solid week (on vacation from the newspaper) in bed drunk. Since I had the week's vacation scheduled, the newspaper knew nothing of my return to the bottle or Charley's absence.

I learned later that this was typical of him. When pressure built up, he would go like a yo-yo from one coast to the other, leaving anyone involved with him stranded. Since I didn't drive, the problem was serious. After the week, I got up out of bed, put the cork in the bottle and shakily returned to work.

GHOST VOICES

That afternoon as I walked down South Virginia Street, a major casino artery, I heard my mother's voice calling me and knew I was getting the DTs. I went into a bar and drank about six large glasses of Coke, causing the bemused bartender to ask me finally, "Is anything wrong?" When I told him I was coming off a week-long drunk, he suggested a "hair of the dog." But I knew that would be fatal.

WET BRAIN

After leaving the bar, I went to Father Charles Shallow's soup kitchen and stood at the head of the line asking not the names but the origin of those seeking food: "Where are you from?" and "What are you doing in Reno?"

Some of the Indians in the line would say, "I come from. . ." and not complete the sentence. I asked the woman in charge if I had offended them and she told me, "No. They have the wet brain and don't know where they come from."

I went back to the paper and wrote my best column while in Nevada, according to most critics. While writing it, I saw a recently deceased friend from the *Journal-American*, a fellow alcoholic, Tom Maloney, whom my children used to call "Mr. Baloney." In the way of the DTs, he actually appeared over my shoulder and told me, "You'll make it. Keep going."

My divorce was final, I couldn't keep my job and the flower shop both going alone, Charley's bills were piling up and I didn't want to risk the children's safety in my distracted state, so I called Terranova, met him in San Francisco, and turned the children over to him for their safety. Anyone who says San Francisco is America's greatest city has never spent the Sunday afternoon I spent there after returning my children to their father. I was totally alone, nearly broke, without a friend in the city and I wandered through the streets in tears until it was time to take the plane back over the Sierra to Reno. Once there, I put in my two weeks' notice and soon after, headed back East to start a new life alone in New York without Charley or the children.

"YOU DON'T WEAR THE PRODUCT!"

My first job was with Bell and Stanton doing public relations for garment center accounts. My first assignment: Maidenform. I saw the children weekends and wrestled, not always successfully, with alcoholism.

A story idea, "The Birth of a Swimsuit," concept by me but story by Gay Pauley of UPI with photographs by Maurice Maurel, hit all over America and Canada, delighting Madame Ida Rosenthal, inventor of the uplift bra and founder and owner of Maidenform. Though she loved my work, she also dryly commented, "But, you don't wear the product!"

Despite this whirlwind start, on the Thanksgiving weekend, lonely and sorry for myself, I got drunk at lunch on the Friday after the holiday and got in a mess.

However, my drinking ended as abruptly as it started. An AA friend, Ray Cudahy, got me into Young and Rubicam where we handled the Travelers Insurance account, setting up their World's Fair exhibit and getting heaps of publicity. I churned out a column—Jean Kinkaid—which went to living section pages, and everything went smoothly until Ray began having some problems. He kept rescinding orders, we found it hard to keep a secretary and I took a cab over to 50 Rockefeller Plaza one day at lunchtime and got hired by the Associated Press, the news organization I have always been most proud of having been associated with.

It was fun and I loved it. I especially liked a guy named Bill Fagan who often sat next to me.

A MORTAL WOUND

A drinker, though not necessarily an alcoholic like myself, he would walk down the long hall on the fourth floor from the major newsroom, take the elevator to the ground floor, the escalator to the underground city, walk about four blocks and then through the subway, coming up at around Eighth Avenue and Forty-Eighth Street in front of a bar called Martin's, where he would have a drink or two and then take his lengthy way back via the Whale Path, as I called it. I said to him one day, "Bill, there's a bar right downstairs."

"I like the companionship," he said. One day, wearing a nice new blue long-sleeved shirt, he put his elbow down on a lighted cigarette, burning a hole in his shirt for sure, maybe his arm.

"Sometimes you wish you would get a mortal wound so you could go home," he told me.

He was upset when his wife rented a cottage on Shelter Island for his summer vacation from 50 Rockefeller Plaza, AP headquarters.

"But it's a beautiful place," I told him.

"It's a mile from the bar," he countered. Though he spent little or no time swimming that summer, he did get a lot of exercise, walking back and forth daily to and from the bar.

FIRST LADY IN NEW YORK

I often covered the First Lady (then Lady Bird Johnson) on visits to New York for AP. Frances Lewin had her in Washington.

The reopening of the newly renovated and refurbished Museum of Modern Art was such an occasion.

During the festivities, Liz Carpenter, her personable press secretary, kept handing me her glass of champagne while attending to her boss. I invariably stowed it on a nearby ledge.

"Are you-all a member of the Anti-Saloon League?" she asked me.

"No, but if a picture showed me holding a glass of champagne, I'd have a lot of explaining to do to my boss, Joe Nicholson," I told her. "Maybe my sponsor, too."

She hung onto the glass herself after that, giving me a conspiratorial wink.

Lady Bird gave me a major beat. I was assigned to cover her attendance at Arthur Miller's play, *After the Fall*, based thinly on his life with Marilyn Monroe. While waiting for her to appear at the Carlyle Hotel where the presidential suite was reserved for the President and his wife, a reporter from UPI arrived and asked my advice, saying she had just come to New York from Boston.

FAIR WARNING

"Watch everyone. But most of all, watch me," I told her. "I'm your competition. From AP."

During the intermission I looked around and noticed that the UPI girl was in the lobby, apparently watching for latecomers. I joined an informal receiving line on the aisle where Mrs. Johnson sat. Joining in the line, I stopped in front of the First Lady and while greeting her and shaking hands, managed to interview her about her reaction to the play, her thoughts about current world situations, whether President Johnson was planning a trip to New York soon, and so forth. She was gracious, and I thanked her and left via a fire door for a phone.

I called 621-1500 and gave the local news desk an exclusive interview, plus an early beat on the straight news of her attendance at the play.

Later, at the Loeb Student Center, seated with Mayor Wagner and Jason Robards, I saw the UPI girl come in. She gave me a look of pure hate. But after all, I had warned her.

My assignments at AP frequently brought me to the powerhouse or the offices of Cardinal Spellman, in back of Saint Patrick's Cathedral. One assignment involved honoring the men who were responsible for the rebuilding of the Church of the Epiphany where my daughter, Sheila, had been baptized. It had been destroyed by an arsonist.

A photographer from the *New York Daily News* told my old friend Monsignor James Asip, now an aide to the Cardinal, that he wanted a narrow picture, just His Eminence and the head of the Carpenters Union.

"Tell him he's come to the wrong man for a narrow picture," was Asip's comment.

I set it up with the union boss at one end, the Cardinal at the other, and all the members who had donated their labor in the middle, so everyone appeared next day in the tabloid.

When I get to New York, I like to visit Saint Patrick's—not for mass or benediction, but just to visit, pray a little and think, maybe light a candle, drop a donation in the poor box. I always look up in the nave for my friend Cardinal Spellman's skullcap. All the cardinals' hats are hung up there.

People were always introducing me to Cardinal Spellman and he would always say, "Oh, Jeanne and I went to Fordham together." He knew I had gone to Fordham Law while I think he attended the university in the Bronx.

THIS WEEK AT TAHOE

Though I have strung for the wire service at many places because of my custody problem, I regretfully left the New York Local Desk of the Associated Press. *Editor and Publisher* had an ad for an editor's job at Lake Tahoe. I took it, though the pay was low, since it would give me a footing.

I interrupted the Donrey Media spokesman when he said that as editor of the *Tahoe Chronicle*, I would handle the money as well as the editorial tasks.

Shaking my head, I carefully stopped him in mid-sentence. "I'm sorry, Sir. I can only be responsible for the editorial content: the writing, headlines, makeup and photo assignments," I told him.

This was agreed to, and it proved to have been a wise stand.

The ads came in and my respect for gamblers grew with them. A handshake was all it took. The check would show up the following day.

Wes, our ad salesman, was a puzzle. He seemed preoccupied. Later I learned that he was a degenerate gambler, one of many I have met. Every payday he headed for Harrah's and gambled all night, returning in the morning broke and tired.

I was musing on Wes while gazing out at the serene lake, surrounded by magnificent pines, when our former landlady in curlers, wearing a red and white check housedress, rushed into the office.

"I'm scared to death," was her preamble. "I've been carrying on a little. I've been such a fool and now I'll have to pay for it! Wes and I have been having an affair, my husband's coming back in a few days from Germany, and I don't know what to do! He doesn't want to end it," she told me.

"Great idiots," I groaned.

Since I had just done an article on a minister across from the paper who had taken a course in marriage counseling, I referred her to the nice padre and hoped for the best. He managed to break up the romance just in time.

IRRATIONAL WES

But Wes bore me a grudge. He blamed me for the breakup. I could tell by the way he kept glaring at me.

A few days later, someone threw a rock through the picture window of the apartment we had moved to in Kelmont East. I knew that Wes had done it.

But his luck ran out. A week or so later, he threw a rock through the window of his former girlfriend's motel as she was showing a room. The prospective tenant was young and fleet of foot. He collared Wes, who was charged with malicious mischief.

"I had to lock up your ad man," Sheriff Crow told me when I went over to represent Donrey Media. "He really is a crackpot. I ordered him to appear here and while I was looking out my window, he attacked the complainant. Threw a punch. Lucky he wasn't killed. I've added assault and battery to the other charge."

"Sheriff! He's a sick man. He's blown all his money at Harrah's, his wife has left him, he's lost his business, and now this!"

I reported having heard that Wes was fairly normal before giving way to his gambling vice. "He needs psychiatry, not jail," was my plea.

AN UNDERWEAR FETISH

Surrounded by rosy satin French undies, teddies, slips and panties trimmed with lace, Sheriff Crow just shrugged. "It's up to the judge now," he replied. "It's on the Circuit Court docket."

He had just captured the Panty Thief. I had run a feature on this, since my own assistant, Dolores, had lost a whole set of new silky undies she and her daughter had given themselves after the father of the family had a big casino win.

The culprit was a fourteen-year-old boy suffering from an underwear fetish. He had stripped all the clotheslines in Tahoe of ladies' underwear, especially if lace-trimmed.

"Yours, Dear?" a burly ski instructor who was there to file a report asked Crow. He then ducked a punch.

ON THE LAM

I was to be very grateful that I'd refused to handle money outside of a petty cash box.

Dick Tiffin, a cameraman, rushed in one morning and asked to replace eighty dollars in that box, saying that the manager had borrowed it. I mused over the absence of an IOU and asked Tiffin to fill out a form, stating that he had returned the money for the other man.

Shortly after this incident, the door opened and in came executives of the Donrey Media Group. "We have a serious problem here with the advertising rates," said the leader.

I held up a hand. "Remember me?" I reminded them. "I don't handle money. I'm strictly editorial."

It turned out that the manager, who had suffered a broken leg and hence couldn't cover his tracks, had been changing ad rates at random and pocketing the difference. By the time they went after him, it turned out he had left the lake, broken leg and all.

Not long after this episode, I wound up my career with Donrey Media and accepted a better job with the Western Scripps League and Chappy Wentworth, my fellow ecologist and nature nut. I never did learn what District Court did about Wes.

WORKING TO SAVE TAHOE

A Dartmouth man, Chapman Wentworth, was my new boss at the *Tahoe Daily Tribune* where I covered stories about the lake and also put out an original feature developed by myself and Charley. It was called "This Week at Tahoe," a show tab, featuring entertainment news of the casinos.

Wentworth, like myself, was a devoted nature lover and zealous conservationist.

The *Tahoe Daily Tribune* was nicknamed "The Sewer News" because the two of us emphasized the need to save the Lake of the Sky from becoming grossly polluted.

"Gentlemen, if Lake Tahoe becomes another stinking Jamaica Bay, you're not going to get the suckers up here," I said at a meeting Wentworth and I had with the top gamblers. After our presentation they arranged to have the solid waste removed from the lake and buried in Truckee, California. Their clout accomplished what no amount of calls, telegrams and articles had done.

"Who's that woman with the two kids who comes through every week with the show tab?" Harvey Gross, owner of Harvey's Casino, asked L. Lew Hardy, his publicist, one day.

"Jeanne Toomey from New York, formerly with the Associated Press," Hardy told his boss.

"Put her on the payroll for a couple of bills a week," Gross ordered. "She can help Will Osborne with the entertainment writing," he went on.

Hardy, chairman of our AA group that met at Harvey's, put me right on the payroll. This extra money was a big help to our budget. I interviewed Tennessee Ernie Ford, Frank Sinatra, Jr., The Three Lads, Charley Shavers and many other show business personalities, turning out lively stories and releases for Harvey's with the knowledge of the *Tribune*.

LIKE A YO-YO

All was well with us until one day Charley disappeared again and left us stranded without a driver. I don't drive since I never got my license, fearing I might drive drunk some day and kill a child. I tried a woman who had lost her job at Saint Theresa's where my children attended school, but she turned out to be another degenerate gambler so I gave up and returned to New York.

AT THE BOOZY HOTEL

Having Charley traced presented few problems since he received a veteran's pension check and I knew someone connected with the V.A.

He sounded really surprised when I ran him down at the Hotel Boozy in Boise, Idaho, told him he was in a good jurisdiction, and asked him to give me a divorce for Christmas. He complied and I became a free woman.

I thought of giving the hotel a testimonial for having a fit name, then wondered if perhaps someone misspelled it for fun.

Jobs were not hard to find. I worked for papers from the edge of the Everglades to Albany, New York, including the *North Port News*, the *Knickerbocker News*, the *Orlando Sentinel*, the *Stamford Advocate*, the *New York Daily News*, the *Philadelphia Journal* and, not to be left out, the *National Enquirer*. Before taking over management of the Last Post Animal Sanctuary, I was editor of the *Calexico Chronicle*, across the border from Mexicali, Mexico.

Because I worked in Nevada and the east coast at different times, there was occasionally a *deja vu* recognition, especially in interviewing entertainers.

In Nevada, for instance, the singer Robert Goulet was telling me a little about himself backstage at Harrah's Casino for an article for the show tab I edited, "This Week at Tahoe," when I noticed he was staring hard at me.

"You look familiar to me," he said. "Have we met before?"

"I covered your wedding to Carol Lawrence for AP at the Plaza Hotel in New York," I said. That made me a friend and he gave me a photo of their firstborn.

Later, back east, I was interviewing Frank Sinatra, Jr. at the Forge in Woodbridge, New Jersey, when I suddenly asked him, "Do you remember me?"

"No. Should I?"

"Do you remember an ice sculpture?" I asked. "It had a light behind it, bringing out the numerals: 21!"

Recognition was immediate.

"My twenty-first birthday—Harvey's Casino, Lake Tahoe!" he remembered.

I nodded, yes.

"You were the news hen!"

I laughed and agreed. I should have cackled. He smiled, and we shook hands.

While working for the *Philadelphia Journal*, I got a friendly "Hello" from an unexpected source, a serial killer, brought into the Round House, Philadelphia's police headquarters, in chains.

I was chatting with the judge, presiding over the court held in the same building, when the City Line Stalker, as the tabloids called him, was brought in for arraignment.

"Hi there!" he called over to me.

"You know him?" asked His Honor, looking nonplussed.

"Well, not what you might call intimately, but I did interview him before he was identified as the killer," I admitted. "He was the lover of the last victim's sister and I talked to both of them, right after the killing. He blamed the crime on bad street lighting!"

"You must be one of the few women he met who is still alive!" commented His Honor.

I felt idiotic admitting this, since we had run my asinine street lighting story while, all along, my prim critic of the City of Brotherly Love's street lighting was the hardhearted murderer of a number of women, including his girlfriend's young sister.

Well, you can't win them all!

I DIDN'T LOVE IKE

Eisenhower was my nemesis. Not through any fault of the 34th president (1953-1961), who died March 28th, 1969. Mainly, my own hangups were responsible.

The first incident actually involved First Lady Mamie Eisenhower. I was covering the launching of the first atomic submarine, the *Nautilus*, on January 21st, 1954, for the Fitzgeralds and NBC Radio.

"Get going, Mamie," I mumbled.

But the First Lady, rumored to be a Scotch drinker, couldn't seem to hit the vessel hard enough to smash the champagne bottle, thus holding up the ceremonies at Groton, Connecticut and killing any hope of my making my deadline.

One down.

The next time was when Eisenhower scheduled a press conference and announced his support for Goldwater. This time the fault was clearly my own, since I had stopped for a drink. When I arrived at the Park Lane, Eisenhower had made a brief statement and retired to an anteroom. Gabe Pressman, formerly of the *New York World-Telegram*, later of NBC-TV, filled me in. I dictated it and it went out immediately over the AP wire. So, I nearly fainted when Eisenhower said, "I didn't say that. You said that!"

After I reminded him that Gabe Pressman had the very same statement, he agreed that he had said it.

My last and very final Eisenhower incident involved his obituary. As wire editor of the *Passaic Herald-News*, I set up a prepared-in-advance obituary with a photograph and headline, framed in black, and was all ready.

Since the latest report indicated that plenty of time remained, I went to lunch.

"Keep the radio on," I asked the composing room crew, always faithful allies. "If he dies, just run the obit and photo. It's all set to go!"

As I was about to enter the coffee shop, I heard "Thirty-Fourth President, World War Two General of the Army Dwight D. Eisenhower is dead."

I ran back, panting, skipped lunch and made sure the presses rolled. I did trust the printers but—best to be sure.

Somehow Eisenhower's demise fit the pattern of a jinx. For me, it seemed a fit conclusion.

Years later, in 1980, Ronald Reagan and Jimmy Carter were seeking the Presidency and I covered both for AP—as a Long Island correspondent.

Dick Roth, formerly of the *Brooklyn Eagle* staff, asked if I wanted to interview the candidate after a lackluster speech by Reagan, whom he represented.

"What's to interview?" I asked.

Carter, who deserves the Nobel Peace Prize, was a more appealing candidate, I thought, though—as an AP reporter—I showed no prejudice. (At least, I hope not.)

My loyalty to AP has led me to call the wire service whenever I encounter anything that seems appropriate. I also work election night regularly in Hartford.

So when in Seattle for the Triennial Convention of the Girl Scouts of America, attired in the green uniform as a media specialist, I knew where my duty lay when Art Linkletter broke down on the stage at the convention center as he told of his daughter's tragic death due to drugs.

Ducking under my desk I busily dialed 212/621-1500 and phoned in a bulletin. A little later, I was primly reviewing Seattle's Visitor's Guide as the *Seattle Times* and *Post-Intelligencer* reporters came by, wondering aloud, "How come AP is already in the office?"

A Girl Scout leader I met there, Lois Johnson, and her husband Robert, are still close friends.

TRANSPORTATION PROBLEMS

It was actually easier to cover for AP in Seattle than on Long Island. Transportation, including the fast special train (developed for the Seattle World's Fair) which connects downtown and the convention center, for instance, is much more available and convenient.

Since I don't drive, getting around as a reporter covering the east end of Long Island required strategy. I took cabs, buses, and sometimes hired a big, jolly and highly intelligent Polish-American named Lottie Adamowitz, who became a friend and drinking companion.

"I'm thick!" she would announce, but she was actually brilliant, and a whiz at math.

We rattled around the South Fork in a huge, ancient limousine, often with me asleep or just passed out in the back seat.

THE COTTON CLUB MURDER

But every Saturday night I usually made the AA meeting at the brown-shingled Methodist Church in Southampton. There I met a most remarkable woman who was to save my life by becoming my sponsor. Renee Dorr was the former wife of the late producer, "Broadway Al" Radin.

Their son, Roy Radin, later was murdered in Gorman, California, victim of the so-called Cotton Club murder. A showman and producer, Roy followed in his father's footsteps and made a fortune. He controlled forty-five percent of the rights to the movie and Robert Evans, the producer, had another 45 percent. Roy stubbornly refused to sell his share to Evans. There were also charges involving cocaine.

Three men, William Mentzer and Alex Marti, the killers and Robert Lowe, the driver, as well as a woman, Lanie Jacobs, were charged with the murder and convicted.

Renee died soon after, ostensibly of cancer but actually of a broken heart. Mainly out of love for her, I attended the pre-trial hearing in Los Angeles. Though the hit men, the driver and the woman who lured Radin to his death were found guilty, Evans, rightly or wrongly suspected by Renee of being the man behind the murder, took the Fifth and was never indicted or charged with anything.

Ironically, the movie turned out to be disappointing, a flop, despite some excellent dancing and top stars.

The curious found it amazing that Renee maintained her sobriety throughout the hunt for her only son, initially reported missing and later, after receiving the terrible news that he had been shot to death in an eerie desert canyon thirteen times because it was Friday, the 13th—May 13th, 1983.

"It would be like spitting in my dead son's face to drink!" Renee told those who marveled at her stoical sobriety.

As a role model, not many arrested alcoholics could match Renee Dorr.

Stringing from the Southampton cottage was like doing piecework in a sweatshop. Money was so sparse as to be negligible. I also yearned for the Christmas-tree glitter of New York, as Gene Fowler once dubbed it.

I left Southampton to help Charley Ward in Stamford where his father, William, was dying. While in Stamford, I hungrily dropped by the local daily, the *Advocate*, applied for a job and was hired as wire editor.

It wasn't long before Charley (I had insanely remarried him, proving how convincing he was and how lonely I was) took off again, leaving me with his aged mother to care for.

I managed to get her into a nursing home, answered an ad in *Editor and Publisher* and wound up working as an articles editor for the *National Enquirer*, then located at Sixtieth Street and Madison Avenue in New York. This experience finally got me out of the red and opened the door to a whole new world of freelancing.

THE NATIONAL ENQUIRER

"Why are you leaving us?" Ted Yudain, editor of the *Stamford Advocate*, had asked on receiving my notice.

"Money!" was the answer, and I tripled my salary by making the switch.

Early on, a major assignment brought me to Brownsville, Texas, to check out a report that then-President Lyndon Johnson's brother had been locked up on drunk-in-public charges and then, because of his brother's high office, been sprung—without appearing in court, paying a fine or going through any of the

142

normal dreary routine.

I found one tough cameraman, Hank Langworthy, who photographed the record and police chief standing in front of the sign, Brownsville Police Department, and a palm tree. Hank delivered me and the prints to the airport. Next morning, back at the *Enquirer* on Madison Avenue, I was congratulated by the boss, Generoso Pope, on a real coup.

The story ran the following week with a front page headline: "LBJ's Brother Arrested as Drunk," and I was queen of the tabloid that week.

After a few lucrative months I quit the full-time job as articles editor when it appeared that my real name would appear in the masthead. I was perhaps stupidly self-conscious about what my AP colleagues might think of me, as well as my family, and elected to freelance for the *Enquirer* and other publications instead, doing interviews with psychiatrists as well as feature stories that fit the formula: medical breakthroughs, analyses of the famous, psychic phenomena, the hero dog and space ships. My byline was Harvey Shapiro, not in any way related to or involving a *Times* man I learned later had that name for real.

PR DAYS

In between newspaper jobs, I managed to pay the rent by working as a flack for various agencies.

Handling a forthcoming exhibition of the work of Alexander Calder was my first important account for the Marianne Strong Agency.

While distractedly involved in setting up his merry-go-rounds and other sculptures at the Perls Gallery, I met him for lunch at the fashionable Carlyle with Gustavus Ober III, Marianne's partner.

Gus and I ordered sober tomato cocktails and waited for Calder to appear.

"A martini!" he ordered when he arrived, easing his huge bulk into a gilt chair and grinning at us two like a slightly tipsy, ruddy Santa Claus.

"Miss Toomey and I are very disappointed in you, Alexander," began Ober.

"Not getting paid?" asked the sculptor with a guffaw.

Looking outraged, Gus Ober continued, "We went to a lot of trouble to get you an interview on a really top NBC television show and, I regret to say, you were too intoxicated to go on!"

Waving to the waiter to bring another martini, Alexander Calder laughed and said, "You know what, Ober, I don't give a damn. I just sold another big sculpture for a million dollars. What do I care about NBC?"

And that was that. We talked of other things and enjoyed our lunch.

I was hard at work very early one morning in my office at Mimi's handsome suite at Eighty-Third and Madison Avenue, doing a piece called "Why Kim Novak Is a Victim of Loneliness and Despair!" for the *Enquirer* (for which I still worked) when the doorbell rang.

Wondering why the doorman had not called us about an early morning visitor, I went to the door, tied up like all New York apartment doors with enough chains for a medieval chastity belt, and yelled through it, "Who is it?"

"Crook!"

"Tony," I called to Mimi's brother, Tony Schappert, who was asleep wrapped in a sheet on an office couch.

"Call the police. They're announcing themselves now!"

"Jane Pemberton—El Paso!" implored the voice.

I recognized that name. She was a stringer of mine for the *Enquirer*.

"Are you from El Paso?"

"Yes!"

A few more shouted inquiries produced the information that the caller was Howard Crook, a writer from El Paso, and that Jane Pemberton had given him my name.

I let him in, got him a temporary job with Mimi and later with UPI and we became lifelong friends. His book, *The Brownstone Cavalry*, a fictional tale of young men after divorce, proves his literary genius. He is now writing another book, this on the Russian mafia in Brighton Beach, which promises to be a bestseller. He lives in Lubbock, Texas, with his delightful wife, Mary Jane.

Mimi and I were agency hostesses to the late Cornelius Vanderbilt Whitney, his wife, Marylou, *New York Post* columnist Earl Wilson and other names in the news at the opening of the then-new Metropolitan Opera, since a client, Bruce Norris, owned the Louis Sherry restaurant at Lincoln Center.

We were all gussied up in evening clothes and I felt quite smugly soignee.

A waiter went by carrying aloft a tray of champagne cocktails. "Oh, don't give any to Jeanne. She's an alcoholic!" warned my boss.

"Why don't you put it on the *Times* tower?" I snarled at her, and left early.

I knew she meant well though, and we remained on friendly terms. Mimi was honestly interested in alcoholism, though she had no problem. (A close family member had been a sufferer.) Thus her understandable reflex.

Society was her beat on the *New York World-Telegram* and the *New York Times*. She was a product of the very social Convent of the Sacred Heart, Mount Saint Vincent and Columbia's School of Journalism.

The billionaire Sam Lefrak, who built Lefrak City, Queens, and other vast housing developments, was among her clients and for a time I edited his weekly paper, *The Long Island Post*, while Mimi presented his daughter, Denise, to society. (She also changed the family name from plain "Lefrak" to the more elegant, in her view at least, "LeFrak.")

Sam had a captive audience for the weekly paper since *The Long Island Post* was distributed to all his apartments. I hired my friend, Phyllis Twachtman, as photographer and we had a merry time being wined and dined at the local bars and restaurants. I ran a dining out column as a regular feature.

Traffic Department Meter Maids hated Phyllis, who would blow a whistle as the uniformed lady traffic officers approached our office in Rego Park. It was wonderful to see the outpouring of drivers from every adjacent building, including the big Lefrak Building on Queens Boulevard. They would collectively move their cars, leaving none to ticket. This cut the ladies' quota, causing them problems back at the station house.

One Saturday we went to Astoria where Lefrak had dispatched us for a layout. We were squired by a gay friend, Dick Gaffney, and some heavy drinking followed. Finally, we went upstairs to a real estate office for a little local history. While there, Phyllis decided that the best angle for photographing the rainy street was to do it upside down. Gaffney held her out the second floor window by her skinny ankles, to the consternation of the real estate personnel.

But we did get a good local angle. At 78-09 Nineteenth Road we found the Rikers Mansion, ancestral home of the family for whom Rikers Island is named. George Washington's surgeon and some early Irish patriots were buried in the back of the house, there were chains in the cellar dating back to slavery, and overall, the visit to Astoria was considered a success. Phyllis's moody blues pictures of the street in rain were of masterpiece quality.

Another Twachtman layout preserved an architectural gem. With Phyllis's superb photos, backed by Carol Taylor's excellent copy, Jefferson Market Court, an unlikely but beguiling Moorish edifice in the heart of the West Village, once the

Women's Prostitution Court and now a public library, was saved from demolition. Both writer and photographer, employed by the *New York World-Telegram and Sun*, were true artists and, fittingly, lived in Greenwich Village.

ORIENT EXPRESS RETURNS

Until she relocated to Newport Beach, California, I enjoyed a stint with Mary Homi Associates, publicizing the fantastic Orient Express, put back on the rails by Jim Sherwood, owner of Sea Containers. He paid for its restoration, buying up old Wagons-Lits cars to fill out the train.

Stories of the maiden rail trips filled the magazines. Only one problem. No one had thought of air conditioning so the wealthy diners sweltered in the dining car on the first (or shakedown) trip. But this was soon corrected. Writing about this legendary railroad train was fun and we hit everywhere with our tales of kings and knaves, jewel thieves and courtesans, princesses and sheiks, card sharps and fortune hunters who in past glory years rode the rails as passengers on the Orient Express.

Mary represented many great hotels of Europe, including the Dorchester, London; the Cipriani, Venice; the Plaza Athenee, Paris, and Brenner's, Baden Baden.

"Mary, we have to call off the clips," I suddenly alerted her one spring day, showing her a news item with the headline "Peter Sellers Is Dead."

"He died at the Dorchester," I went on. Though we called Luce and Burrelle's at once, it was too late. We had to dispose of barrels of news items about the death of the comedian in one of Mary's hotel accounts, hardly desirable publicity.

Mary Homi was and is an elegant woman and a rare boss, always urbane and charming, my all-time favorite female employer.

NOT WASHINGTON'S MOUNT VERNON

Editor and Publisher, journalism's trade journal, led me to many bizarre areas through its Help Wanted columns (invaluable to a wanderer like me). Perhaps the funniest job I ever had was that of Assistant City Editor of the *Mount Vernon Argus* in Westchester County, New York, far from George Washington's Mount Vernon.

I enjoyed every minute I worked there. Reporting at six in the morning daily, I dashed out at two in the afternoon and made the 2:03 to New York where I edited Jerry Finkelstein's "New York Column" on Lower Broadway. He published the *New York Law Journal* and a civil service trade paper, the *Civil Service Leader*, in the same skyscraper.

Racial tensions sometimes made Mount Vernon appear like a war zone. Cursed with the desire to reveal "the true city" wherever I'm at, I sometimes took my then-sixteen-year-old son, Peter, to Mount Vernon. One day I led him down Fourth Avenue to a storefront spiritualist church.

Peter studied a large aquarium tank which occupied a prominent place in the ground floor operation. "I didn't know that you could keep cold water fish like these goldfish in with tropicals, Reverend," Peter politely remarked to the handsome African-American minister.

"They have to learn to live together!" roared the clergyman, with a big winning smile.

A former barn with nine wings on First Avenue on the south side of Mount Vernon was the home at one time of a Hudson River artist, Edward Gay. Behind the living room door, this cheerful philosopher painted "his" ship, which was always coming in. When the plaster over his mantel cracked, he painted a string of singing blackbirds. Over his tub he painted the ocean on one wall and a lake on the other. In every corner appeared a tiny work of art: a dragonfly, a robin's nest, a butterfly, or perhaps my favorite, an owl.

At the head of the stairs appeared a large framed photograph of an impressive looking lady. Below it a handwritten inscription read, "To the gentleman who has the honor of being the husband of Mrs. Edward Gay."

If it's possible to fall in love with a dead man, I truly love Edward Gay, his gift of laughter and what he accomplished, including donating the murals in the Mount Vernon Library. I wrote features on the house for the *Argus* and later on for the *Knickerbocker News* in Albany during my tenure there as People's Editor.

Edward Gay is buried in nearby Saint Paul's churchyard. His grave is marked by a handsome wrought iron bench designed by an artist daughter employed by Tiffany's. The visitor may rest a while and study the line from Milton's

"Lycidas" which this remarkable man selected before his death: "Tomorrow to fresh woods and pastures new."

GLUE SNIFFER

The janitor and I were the first arrivals at the *Argus* (named for the giant of a thousand eyes). On a drab grey morning in the winter of 1972, we had a visitor.

"May I help you?" I asked.

"I'se looking for some glue to sniff," our visitor said.

Nodding at the janitor, a signal to alert the police, I murmured, "Well, you've come to the right place. Help yourself!" At the same time I pointed to the copy desk which featured pots of paste for making up pages.

Our boss, a good-looking ex-Navy man, Bob Merriss, came breezily in. Looking over at the stringbean in a long black coat, busily sniffing, he shrugged inquiringly.

"Oh, he wanted some glue to sniff," I explained, hastily adding, "We accommodated him. They're coming." A uniformed Mount Vernon policeman next appeared, and I explained again, adding, "He can keep the glue. We've got plenty."

My next port of call in 1972 was to be the *Orlando Sentinel*, where I worked briefly while Disney's Never-Never Land was rising on a nearby swamp. Though it seems disloyal to the American dream, as a conservationist I much preferred the swamp.

In Orlando, my first major assignment was reporting the reinstitution of the death penalty. I interviewed a former Raiford warden and enjoyed touring Orlando with him.

"Hello! How are you, Warden?" a roofer called down from a lofty peak.

"One of my success stories," the former prison head told me, waving up to his former charge and yelling, "Glad to see you, Joe."

He was greeted by several men he had known at Raiford and properly took pride in their apparent rehabilitation.

But the sirens of booze were whispering to me and I started sneaking into the Palm Garden, a nearby bar. Here I met Jim Gray, a former Cleveland cop and my fourth and last husband. With my alcoholism back in action, I soon left

Orlando and went home with Jim.

We married and returned to Florida later, putting out a weekly, the *North Port News*, on the sleepy Gulf Coast of the Sunshine State. While there I sold articles to the *National Enquirer*, *Modern Maturity*, and Florida magazines. It was fun but I continued to pore over the Help Wanted ads since money was tight, and the summers promised to be very hot, though not as hot as a later destination, Calexico, where natives sum up, "It's where the sun spends the winter, and fools spend the summer."

FLEEING THE TROPICS

I got a response to an ad seeking a People's Editor in Albany.

"You're a great writer," Managing Editor Jack Pease of the *Knickerbocker News* said when we met at a Raleigh hotel to discuss my application. "But you're not drinking anymore, are you?" he gently asked.

I realized he would know my history since the *Knickerbocker News*, like the *Journal-American* and King Features Syndicate, were owned by the Hearst Corporation.

Well, I could truthfully say that I wasn't drinking then and I was hired.

Until my final collapse there, I ran a lively department and made some wonderful friends, including Kathleen Condon, a former nun, who was my competent, funny, superb assistant.

Stunting was a specialty. My proudest feat may have been to bring a noted astrologer to the track.

"I betrayed my gift," she said in explanation of why she bombed out worse than I did at the betting window, even though she brought her crystal globe with her. The *Knickerbocker News* ran an outstanding picture with the story, showing the horses flashing by, clearly reflected in the globe. This stunt was equalled another time when I ran a picture of our "Track Tips" editor for the New York Column. The horses were reflected in his eyeglasses.

"But don't you prostitute your gift when you charge fifty dollars a reading?" I cattily asked the mystic. No answer.

In AA it is well and truly said that if you have a slip, you will do so at the worst possible time.

In Albany, calamity struck as I prepared to cover for the Living Department the social event of the season, the Saratoga Ball for the Performing Arts.

Though I ordered a new gown and planned to look reasonably chic, once I picked up a drink I forgot all about it. I never did pick up my dress. Instead, I arrived at the party in a bedraggled long black velvet skirt, leftover from Mimi Strong's wardrobe, and a dismal middy blouse.

"Retire from the field of battle. Go to the field hospital," my King Features colleague Joan O'Sullivan always warned me—to no avail.

Though bleary-eyed, I still could see the woman I had replaced, the late Kay Harrington, looking my way with an expression of triumphant joy.

"Has she been sticking a voodoo doll with pins?" I asked myself.

No matter. I did it to myself. So ended my stint in Albany.

But I saved all the memos, suggesting an immediate departure.

"You quit!" the State Unemployment interviewer in Bridgehampton told me when I returned home to the Hamptons and applied for benefits. Handing him the memos, I replied, "Not exactly. Take a look."

"You qualify," he acknowledged. Back home at the cottage in Southampton I decided to return to college, obtaining my long-delayed B.A. in 1976. (When I went to law school, only two years of college were required.) I received my last check on the same day I started a new job in Woodbridge, New Jersey.

STRINGING FOR EVERYBODY

Through the years, Jim and I occasionally strung for the Associated Press and assorted weeklies from home base, the Hamptons.

Nancy Willey of Sag Harbor, a local historian and wit, christened us an editorial version of Bonnie and Clyde. We often worked for the late great-hearted, if eccentric, Victoria Gardner, long-time publisher of the *Sag Harbor Express*, now owned by Gardner Cowles and edited by the dedicated Bryan Boyhan, a supporter of all locals including journalists.

From 1976 to 1986 I wrote a column called "Sidelights" for the *Woodbridge News Tribune* in New Jersey. It is now merged with the *New Brunswick Home News*.

A dog led to my being employed there. Jim was running the Dutch Motel in Woodbridge for the financial wizard John Victor Agar. A couple and their dog were stranded and I, typically, sought help for the dog. I called the newspaper, was turned over to the publisher and after listening to me, good-hearted John W. Burk sent over both food and money for the couple and a case of dog food for Gwennie, the dog, a reddish mixed breed, possibly part Irish setter.

He also generously paid their motel bill.

"Tell me about yourself," he asked.

"Well, I've worked for a lot of newspapers," I told him, pulling out clips to prove it.

After listening to a synopsis of my rambling editorial history, he said with a nice smile, "Well, you've worked everywhere else. Would you like to work here?"

"I would like to very much," I answered.

Studying my clips, he was especially taken by the Reno columns. While the name of my *Reno Evening Gazette* column, "Sierra Sidelights and Reno Insights," hardly fit a New Jersey daily, he showed interest in the format.

"We'll just call it "Sidelights," he said, and I was hired and broke my own record, staying with the paper for ten years. And stayed cold sober. Sobriety has its rewards. While working for the *News-Tribune*, we acquired a pleasant house with a swimming pool in Point Pleasant on the Jersey shore.

Since, luckily for me, I arranged my own hours and thus could write the column when it seemed best, I managed to again follow Sam's example and worked for other papers, too, as well as doing some publicity work.

This made for an extensive work week, including a daily commute by train, back and forth to Thirtieth and Market in Philadelphia where for some months I worked for the tabloid *Philadelphia Journal*.

ANGELO BRUNO'S WAKE

"Bruno's been killed. Here's one for you, Liz," city editor Walt Herring called over to me. "Go get 'em," he yelled.

I was in back of the city room, interviewing Joey Bishop who was upset over a column item hinting that he had cancer.

"I was visiting a friend who is sick," Bishop explained. "I'm fine." I promised we'd run a correction, and said my good-byes to one of Philadelphia's best loved personalities.

Angelo Bruno, Philadelphia's godfather, was laid out in a Broad Street funeral home, Herring told me. I went over there and walked right in.

As the world's worst dresser, I outdid even my usual disastrous lack of style, wearing a green coat picked up at a thrift shop in Florida and a non-matching babushka.

I think I was taken for some neighborhood fixture from South Philadelphia, the type who loves wakes and attends all of them, like my late grandmother. No one bothered me so I went into the chapel and sat in front of the coffin. The general layout made me think of Knocko Minnihan's wake in Edwin O'Connor's *The Last Hurrah*. The cost of the flowers alone would have paid the *Journal*'s rent for a month.

I walked quietly around for a few minutes, studying all the largest pieces. One outstanding arrangement featured huge yellow calla lilies and was signed by a thug known as "Chicken" Testa. I tried to memorize the names without taking any notes and returned to my seat.

"Who are you?" suddenly demanded a sleek peroxide blond in a smart black suit topped by a mink coat. Enough gold chains hung from her to tie up the Queen Elizabeth II.

She headed a group of well-dressed Italian-American ladies. Waves of Chanel Number Five enveloped me.

"I'm Mrs. Terranova," I said. "He was such a good man!" I went on, respectfully, indicating the corpse. The deferential attitude and the Italian name worked and they left me to my thoughts.

It was dark when I left, coming down the steps behind a top labor leader.

"Hey, Liz" (my name in Philadelphia), yelled one of my colleagues, all held back behind barricades.

I ran my finger around my throat, glared, and leaped into a passing cab, returning to the *Journal* to write my impressions of gangland's farewell tribute to Angelo Bruno.

After the story ran under my Philadelphia byline, Liz Gray, I received a highly critical letter from one of the fashionably-turned-out ladies.

I replied at once, praising Italian culture, including music, art, architecture and cuisine, and pointing out that, far from being anti-Italian, I was married to the late Deputy Chief Inspector Peter Terranova, my children are partly of Italian descent, and I love everything Italian except criminals.

I heard no more about Angelo. All the men who sent those big floral pieces have since been murdered.

There was one stunt I couldn't carry out, though. I had a trick camera in my purse, but I was under too much observation to even try it.

Working in Philadelphia was fun and I hated to drop my daily commute, but the Palmetto I took nightly got later and later until, instead of leaving the station at Thirtieth and Market Streets at nine o'clock, it was chugging out at eleven and even later. I couldn't get enough sleep to keep it up, so I regretfully gave Editor Walt Herring my resignation.

I kept in touch with Jody Kolodzey, the entertainment editor, though. She still calls me "Liz."

GIANT OF THE JERSEY SHORE

During the ten years on the *News-Tribune*, I also did some copyreading and features for the *Asbury Park Press*, trying to avoid any overlapping by writing stories about people and events outside of the *News-Tribune*'s circulation area. However, apparently this was not enough and objections were voiced. I had to make a decision and chose to stay on the Woodbridge daily because I was near retirement and a modest pension. It was not an easy choice, since I really liked the *Press*, especially their cafeteria, and it was right near home.

ATTEMPT AT RETIREMENT

In 1986 I "retired" to New Mexico, joined the Albuquerque Press Club, did a few travel pieces, and kept in touch with newspaper friends like Kathleen Casey, most recently travel editor of the *Newark Star-Ledger*. She visited New Mexico with her then-husband Mark while we were living there.

After accompanying Kathleen and Mark to Gran Quivira and other historic ruins, including cliff cities, and attending the Santa Fe Opera to see Puccini's *Madama Butterfly*, I suggested that we visit Taos. We took the high road from Española, stopping off at the Santuario de Chimayó.

Called the Lourdes of New Mexico, the sanctuary has a dry well. By reverently taking some of this earth and, of course, praying that an intention may be granted, many claim that their prayers have been answered. Testimonial letters, canes and crutches are displayed. It is a popular stopping-off place for tourists.

We made a brief stop at Chimayó. I followed the ritual, asking for a favor, and we resumed our trip.

At Taos it began to rain, a light silvery rain, somewhat curtailing our sightseeing. I asked Kathleen if she would like to visit the *Taos News*, owned and published by Robin McKinney Martin, daughter of the publisher of the *Santa Fe New Mexican*, Robert McKinney, sometimes called the Wizard of Wall Street.

Kathleen expressed interest and we went right over to the *Taos News*, a state-of-the-art weekly, located in a handsome plant with exotic landscaping featuring apricot trees. Though I did not expect to see Robin, who was near term in her first pregnancy, the clerk at the desk told me, "Robin's in and she'd like to see you."

Kathleen accompanied me. After introductions, Robin asked, "Jeanne. How would you like to edit a paper for me in California?"

"I'd love to!"

"It goes to 130 degrees in the summer," she warned.

"I don't care if it goes to ten below zero," I told her. "I'm dying to go back to work."

In a few weeks I became editor of the *Calexico Chronicle*, located on the Mexican border across from Mexicali, Mexico.

Without making too much of it, I've often mulled over this incident. My secret intention at Chimayó was, of course, to get a job.

AMERICA'S SALAD BOWL

Editing a weekly in Calexico showed me a whole new world. Tiny Calexico, with a population of some nineteen thousand, swells to sixty thousand every night. Some forty thousand Mexicans come across the border from Mexicali via the port of entry at two o'clock in the morning to pick the vegetables that make the Imperial Valley America's winter salad bowl.

Women wash the vegetables in great rocky ships of the desert, great open carts on wheels, seal them in plastic wrappers, and they're ready for supermarket shelves throughout the world.

Considering unemployment in the northwest in particular, which lumbermen claim necessitates continuing the destruction of century-old trees and the denuding of the Olympic Peninsula, I wonder why Americans cannot be found to earn from two to five hundred dollars weekly, plus benefits, as pickers; but everyone there says that Americans just will not stoop to do stoop labor!

The late Cesar Chávez, who organized the Campesinos, came to Calexico and I covered his visit, which culminated in a parade through Calexico with the workers whose lives he had enriched.

A 6.6 earthquake hit Calexico in November of 1987. While it caused some structural damage, there were no deaths in our town. A woman and child in Mexicali were killed when a driver lost control of his car during the quake.

Jim and I love Calexico, and plan to visit it again and see Rosa Nogueda, my assistant, and other friends—like Luis Hernandez, who operated a modest animal shelter with his own funds, keeping a plastic tub full of water in each dog's kennel to provide comfort in the heat. But the cost of air conditioning plus rent made a permanent stay financially impossible. The earthquake gave us food for thought, too, since we now know that three faults, the Westminster, Superstition Mountains and the famous one, the San Andreas, all meet there.

So we were there only six months, from Labor Day 1987 to March 1988 and then reluctantly left for New Jersey, carrying three cats and three dogs in the back of the Blazer. One cat, named Quake, was born in that November 1987 earthquake.

MADAME DE STAEL

I quit my first post in Newark, churning out business news for a government office, in a few weeks after learning that my boss, who shall be nameless, was preoccupied with Madame de Stael (1766-1817), author and sworn enemy of Napoleon. She also required every release to be rewritten on the average of twenty-seven times.

Thanks to another wonderful newspaperman, Frederick J. Kerr, Managing Editor for News of the *Asbury Park Press*, I connected right away, again helping to edit the Community section of the "Giant of the Jersey Shore," as the *Press* was billed. I was much relieved to be back east on a daily newspaper with a generous payroll again.

A CAREER CHANGE

In January 1989, my old friend and one-time employer Pegeen Fitzgerald died. The assignment to supervise the operation of her Last Post Animal Sanctuary in rural northwestern Connecticut followed. At this writing I am still on the job as chief of operations and concierge of a cat hotel and retirement home.

We are greeted mornings with chirps, whoops, squawks, coos, songs, shrieks, screams and screeches by a wide variety of birds, since the animal home is located on the Housatonic River. We shelter two hundred seventy-five cats, two miniature goats, three pot-bellied pigs, four rabbits, a few retired dogs and one spoiled guinea pig. There are deer, wild turkeys, raccoons and opossums on the grounds. It is a paradise for both domestic and wild creatures.

ECONOMIC SURVIVAL

Besides having learned from Sam Rubenstein the technique of adding human interest details to make a front page story out of a routine assignment, I mastered the art of economic survival in a volatile industry which, when I joined it, was about to enter a life-and-death struggle for the advertising dollar with the mighty newcomer: television.

Most of the newspapers once represented at Bergen Street, including my alma mater the *Brooklyn Daily Eagle*, lost the battle.

Thanks to Sam's example and training, I learned early the wisdom of having more than one job at a time. I frequently managed to double up.

Among the newspapers I worked for were: the *Passaic Herald-News*, the *Mount Vernon Daily Argus*, the *Orlando Sentinel*, the *North Port News*, the *Dover*

Advance, the *Philadelphia Journal*, *Asbury Park Press*, *Ocean County Observer*, *Stamford Advocate*, *Point Pleasant Leader*, *Woodbridge News Tribune* and the *Calexico Chronicle*.

Public relations affiliations included Howard Rubenstein's, where I won the Silver Fox award for a splashy *New York Times* story I placed for the Jewish Guild for the Blind.

I enjoyed the heady atmosphere of Howard's thriving agency in the Mill Building, just north of the Hilton. But the biggest thrill of all was seeing again my old teacher and survival guide, Sam Rubenstein, who was working there with his son. Sam had formed my life as much as my favorite book, George Santayana's *The Last Puritan*, had developed my philosophy.

Not long after working for Howard on a few projects, I learned that Sam was dead. The headline on the *New York Post* read only "Ruby Is Dead."

Every veteran newsman in the city knew who Ruby was. I took a cab to the railroad, caught the first train into New York and attended his simple funeral at the Riverside Funeral Home, Seventy-Sixth Street and Amsterdam Avenue. There were no flowers, no music. Sam died as he lived, a man of strong principles, enormous integrity and modest faith. He was, I assume, Orthodox, strictly conforming to the rites and traditions of Judaism. I saw Howard coming down the aisle wearing a yarmulke, and bowed. None of the men I once worked beside at Bergen Street were there. Almost all of those newsmen whose bylines were once a household word were dead.

How proud Sam must have been of Howard, I thought.

Death comes sooner or later to every man. But Sam's final hours must have given him peace in the sure and certain knowledge of a life well spent.

Some people light up a room when they enter it. I've had the privilege of knowing people who lit up my life in the same way while they were here: Sam Rubenstein, Eddie Mahar, Joe Nicholson, Phyllis Twachtman, my poetess mother Gene O'Grady, and chemist (and during Prohibition, bootlegger) father Edward Aloysius Toomey, Jane Corby, Helen Worth, George Mills and so many others.

Their light shone bright and clear and, sadly, quite often that kind of light burns fast.

In some small way I've tried to tell some of their stories and what it was like when newspapers attracted the brightest and the best, when linotype machines roared and rattled the press rooms of the great newspapers, like the *Journal-American* on South Street, and when STOP THE PRESSES heralded the need to hold everything and remake the front page. (My son, Peter Terranova, contributed ideas, including this tribute to former colleagues).

EPILOGUE

My only School of Journalism was school papers.

Seeing the sign, Owl Printing, from a car window on Sunrise Highway in Rockville Center, Long Island, the other day brought it all back, my first school newspaper experience as Feature Editor of Long Beach High School's *The Long Beach Tide*, and how that hands-on experience saved me from displaying total ignorance when I landed my first real newspaper job at twenty-one in 1943.

With Janice Vogel, the editor, it was my duty to bring the *Tide* via bus from Long Beach to Rockville Center, Long Island, to be printed by The Owl.

No editor was ever prouder than myself when, as though by magic, the paper came out at regular intervals, recounting what passed for news at any high school: plays, scholarships, sports, faculty interviews and staff changes.

The next news reporting experience was gained on my college paper, *The Hofstra Chronicle*, where I was Exchange Editor and wrote a column called "Personality Quiz."

I had no other newspaper training or experience when, at the suggestion of my best friend Virginia Henschel (later Mrs. John Deraval), who lived in Brooklyn, I applied for a job on the *Brooklyn Daily Eagle* after the New York papers had ignored my pleas. (The *Eagle* was hiring women because of the wartime shortage of young active men.)

I had tried to keep up with my ambition to become a lawyer by working for a year as a law clerk for Cardozo and Nathan at One Wall Street, Manhattan. But at twelve dollars a week, it seemed unlikely that I was going to earn enough to pay tuition at law school. One year as a nineteen-year-old at Fordham Law School, then located in the Woolworth Building at 233 Broadway, was all I had. I passed, but was totally broke.

At least I never got involved in a libel suit. One of my first-year courses was criminal law, including libel law.

SAFE STREETS

There was freedom in the forties because of the safety of the streets and subways in those long-gone days. I took the IRT from Borough Hall, Brooklyn, home to Greenwich Village in the middle of the night and never had a problem. Blanche Krell, a brilliant, dramatically dark and witty musician, Shirley Krasnof, a lively sociologist with a striking figure, and I shared a furnished apartment on West Fourth, corner of Jane Street in the heart of the West Village. We split the rent of $47.50 a month.

We met first at the Alma Matthews House, a Methodist residence club on West Eleventh Street in the heart of Greenwich Village, which had a quota of two Jewish and two Catholic girls. Blanche and Shirley were the two Jewish girls and I was the Catholic half. The Methodists were wonderful. They never tried to convert us and were kindness itself. However, they had one requirement. Residents had to have supper at home a certain number of nights every week. Blanche went on the road as a professional musician, I got assigned to the *Eagle*'s nightside staff, and Shirley had too many dates. We had to find an apartment.

I overheard Blanche ask Shirley one day why I always brought home a bottle of Myers rum every payday and kept it under the sink.

"It's an Irish cultural pattern," replied our resident sociologist.

I thought I drank to open what Aldous Huxley called "the doors to perception." But hitting bottom and being educated about the drug, alcohol, in hospitals and AA, made it clear I was just another suffering drunk.

One day at a time has kept me sober for twenty-two years, hopefully forever.